TRAINING SPANIELS

Joe Irving

DAVID & CHARLES
Newton Abbot London North Pomfret (Vt)

British Library Cataloguing in Publication Data

Irving, Joe
    Training spaniels.
    1. Spaniels
    2. Dogs – Training
    I. Title
    636.7'52   SF429.S7

    ISBN 0–7153–8008–7

First published 1980
Second impression 1982

Printed in Great Britain
by Biddles Ltd   Guildford   Surrey
for David & Charles (Publishers) Limited
Brunel House   Newton Abbot   Devon

Published in the United States of America
by David & Charles Inc
North Pomfret   Vermont 05053   USA

Contents

Foreword

I purchased my first gun dog, a springer spaniel, in 1963, and from that moment on my life-style changed. I had answered an advertisement in the local paper announcing that a professional gun-dog trainer had a first-class trained spaniel of impeccable breeding for sale, reasonable to a good shooting home. I was pretty wet behind the ears in those days where dogs were concerned and it must have shown, for I was given a demonstration of the dog's prowess in about five minutes flat. This demonstration consisted of the 'trainer' throwing a rabbit-skin dummy once, whereupon the dog rushed out, picked and brought it to hand. Green as I was, I remember quite clearly that the man had to use both hands to prise open this paragon of virtue's mouth to extract the dummy. Nevertheless I bought the dog. No instructions were given, just a shake of the hand and a 'Best of luck, sir, he's a wee topper.' I was to learn all too swiftly just what a 'wee topper' he was.

Within the next six or seven weeks this dog was to push me to the very limits of human endurance, as he illustrated only too convincingly just how first-class his training had been. He ran into flush, both fur and feather, careered into the wide blue yonder whenever a shot was fired, hunted for most of the day 'in the next parish', and on the few occasions that I managed to get a shot, delivered the game well and truly gralloched. Yet, for all his shortcomings I think I loved the little brute, and consequently was prone to making excuses for him.

Finally in desperation I took him to a local gamekeeper who had a good reputation for training gun dogs. Thus I met Hardie Carruthers of Orchardton, one of the most honest and friendly men I have ever met, certainly the most patient, for I must have appeared the most 'undoggy-wise' of people to him. Many times over the years I have thought back with acute embarrassment at the things I must have said to him, the excuses I made for the dog, whilst Hardie patiently tried to get through to me just what a hopeless case 'Skip' was. In the end I got the message and gave the dog away to an old lady who lived on a small island on the west coast of Scotland, where there were no roads and a proliferation of rabbits. She just wanted a dog for company, and I like to think that she got what she wanted for he was a lovable little fellow for all his faults, and that he lived out his allotted span in this spaniel paradise.

On Hardie's advice I bought a little bitch of 8 weeks old, and raised her until she was 6 months old in the company of another dog puppy which I bought to keep her company, because she howled at night. Thus many readers will recognise an all too familiar pattern emerging, one no doubt they have experienced themselves. Doubtless many still do and, probably feeling that the situation is hopeless, are resigned to just accepting it, but they should read on and take heart.

'Pip', for that was her name, was a daughter of field-trial champion 'Breckonhill Bilko' and 'Rivington Maechele' – first-class, nay impeccable, breeding. Whilst Hardie trained her at his kennels, I bumbled along with her erstwhile kennel-mate 'Dandy' with the aid of the gun-dog text-book of the day, and in retrospect made not too bad a job of him, finally selling him for the princely sum of £80 when 'Pip' returned from Hardie. In six months he had worked what to me was pure magic. He gave me an intensive demonstration of her capabilities and, I now realise, a schooling session for my personal benefit. In his inimitable way, with extreme tact and diplomacy, he showed me what to do and what not to do, whilst he put her through her paces.

Over the next few months my shooting forays were to take on a new dimension. Never before had walked-up game been served up to my gun with such efficiency. I now know that 'Pip' deteriorated due to my ignorance and mishandling, but a short 'refresher' at Hardie's was sufficient for me to be able to take her into a novice trial at Strathardle and win a certificate of merit. Thus the bug had bitten, I couldn't wait to experience the thrill of competition again, and so my field trial career began. I never ever won a trial with 'Pip' through no fault of hers. She suffered from my inexperience but nevertheless taught me a lot. Her puppies have gone all over the world, five of them winning trials in this country. After a full and happy life, she went to sleep in 1977, an unforgettable friend.

Since those early days I have trained gun dogs in ever increasing numbers, and of almost every breed. A few were brilliant, most were adequate, and of course there were the inevitable failures which the laws of average put our way. Some trainers are reluctant to admit to them, but if we are honest, we must. In the training of gun dogs, more so perhaps than in most pursuits, an invaluable asset to the trainer is the ability to look inwardly, to understand himself and his own shortcomings, to recognise when the mistakes are his, and to learn and profit from them.

It is this gift of insight, coupled with the ability to understand a dog, that differentiates the trainer from the breaker. The trainer realises his own faults, takes the trouble to assess his pupil's temperament and, without clouding his judgement with sentiment, acts accordingly. On the other hand the breaker, generally speaking, tends to be totally oblivious to his own faults. He knows it all, and consequently is incapable of learning, relying solely on his ability to batter a dog into submission. Breakers are scornful of the sensitive dog, purely because their methods are totally useless with this type of pupil. Whilst the trainer's ratio of failures tends to be small, the breaker's failures on the other hand far exceed his successes.

My own methods of training a dog are, as any method must be, based on the fundamentals evolved through the years by men who have gone before, most of whom are now completely forgotten. Most of them, good or bad, contributed in some way to the writings of their times. Some used the word 'psychology' in what they wrote – all credit to them, for they had stumbled on the secret of successful training. I say 'stumbled', for at the time when they wrote, psychology was an infant science; they could not appreciate it, far less implement it fully, and consequently only scratched its surface. It is only in the last three decades that psychology has come into its own in the treatment of humans. The psychological approach to the training, indeed the understanding, of the canine mind, was not fully realised until even more recently.

There are many ways in which a dog's thinking processes differ from ours, but I do not believe they differ to a great degree. I am convinced that, so long as allowances are made for the dog's limited powers of comprehension, and he is handled with consistency and patience, anyone can train a dog to that particular dog's full potential. Any parents capable of providing a stable environment for their children are perfectly capable, with a little guidance, of training a dog. The fundamentals are the same. A dog, as with a child, must know his behavioural boundaries, he must know what behaviour will be accepted and what will not be tolerated, and this can only be achieved by consistency tempered with understanding. There is only one way to teach a dog to sit, that is to utter the command, 'sit', and initially show the dog what you mean by demonstration. There are slight variations of this theme, but basically that's it. The same argument for consistency applies to almost every aspect of training.

The methods of training as laid down in this book differ greatly in some ways from those of my predecessors. For having studied psychology in relation to disturbed children for many years before I became involved in training dogs, I found after the first few dogs had passed through my hands, that my style of training gradually changed until I was using the same methods to train a dog that I used with the children, and enjoying a far greater ratio of success.

Throughout this book I shall attempt to envisage the many problems that beset the trainer, and offer solutions to each aspect of training. For no dog, or for that matter trainer, is born perfect and the novice must be able to find out the answers to his queries if there is to be any hope of success.

And the queries are many. For instance, one trainer tells us that he prefers a hard dog and has little time for the sensitive one; another tells us that the sensitive dog, if brought along gently at his own pace, will at the end of the day be worth his weight in gold, for he will look upon you as his God and do for you because he lives to please you and you alone. Why does one trainer advocate one type of dog and another the opposite, and yet each be highly successful with his chosen pupils? May I hazard a guess, albeit an informed one, and say that it is because, having tried various temperaments, they found that

7

whilst they enjoyed success with one type they failed, or at least had to work hard on, the other, finally concluding that their particular choice was the best – a natural enough assumption on their part. Each trainer discovered that such and such a temperament is suited to his own individual personality, consequently a hard dog will blossom in the hands of a hard trainer, whereas a more sensitive animal will quickly become frightened with the methods he employs. The sensitive dog will respond to a far higher degree in the hands of a person less forceful; the bolder type in such an environment may quickly take over and become a wild uncontrollable brute.

Thus the novice trainer seeking advice may well find he is confronted with opinions that vary enormously. What is he to do? Who is he to believe? In fact all viewpoints are correct. But over the years, trainers' particular techniques evolve and become stylised. Therefore their opinions become narrow, each does not like another's type, each is of the opinion that he is right and therefore another is wrong. Their convictions are coloured by their own experience, naturally so, but it is very confusing to the layman.

This book is written on the premise that it is not difficult to train a dog, provided some form of guidance is available. I have tried as far as possible to keep everything simple without avoiding the complexities of the subject and I hope I have provided something useful for the layman who can, I believe, train a spaniel of suitable intelligence, no matter what its temperament, to a highly creditable standard. He will understand his dog and his own individual temperament a little better, and thereby discover that it is just as easy to instill good habits and enjoy their benefits, as it is to instill bad habits and suffer from them. If you follow this book step by step, you will learn how to develop a puppy from 8 weeks old, preparing him for training at approximately 6 months old through to a highly trained working dog, indeed to field trial standard if you wish, providing your dog has the necessary inherent qualities.

Without a rabbit pen – although the construction of a simple inexpensive version is included for the reader who wishes to build one – or any special gimmicks, you will be shown how to steady a dog to fur and feather, how to train him to handle out to a blind retrieve with whistles and hand signals, how to teach him to follow and retrieve a runner, to retrieve from land or water, quarter his ground within shot at all times, and much more.

Most professional trainers that I have met, unlike myself, started out as gamekeepers, and consequently had the most important asset of all – unlimited facilities, both in ground and distribution of game. In such circumstances the training of a dog is much easier, there is no doubt of that. Very rarely will you see a gamekeeper with a young, what is known in the trade as a 'sticky', dog, that is a dog which lacks the confidence to hunt. This book, however, was not written for the professional, or for the semi-professional such as the gamekeeper, but for the novice, who perhaps suffers as I did for many years from lack of ground and, even more importantly, game. In these circumstances one has to use one's ingenuity to improvise, so that a creditable standard of training may be attained. Should the reader be fortunate enough to have access to suitable facilities, it will make the task ahead that much easier and more interesting.

However, therein lies the most common danger of all to the inexperienced dog handler – the temptation to get on. It is so easy to skimp the early training in one's eagerness to get on to more interesting exercises, to introduce the dog to game too soon, thereby putting temptation in his path before the training is firmly enough embedded in his mind. Thus bad habits are instilled; habits which may prove impossible or very difficult to eradicate, almost certainly involving a great deal of work that could have been avoided by exercising a little patience. Therefore, if you have to work hard for every head of game, don't be discouraged. For if through lack of it you dwell on the early training a little longer, your dog will be that much better equipped to deal with temptation when it does come his way.

Owing to the many different circumstances, hereditary qualities and, by no means least, the temperament of both the dog and the trainer, a particular animal may react entirely differently to a given situation than any other. Intelligence, aptitude, interpretation and experience, all will come into play, to the extent that even litter brothers and sisters may react in a wide variety of ways.

Let me make it quite clear that there is no difference whatsoever in the training of a shooting dog to that of a dog destined to run in field trials. This is a myth, the origins of which are something of a mystery to me, and which should be exploded. For not only does it give rise to confusion, it affords an excuse for not training a dog properly. Content to make do, the owner rather than expend time and energy during the off season, glibly remarks on seeing his dog commit every crime in the book on a shooting day, 'Oh, he's just a shooting dog.' Not to put too fine a point on it, the dog who does not behave himself on a shoot is a pest, not only to the owner but to all and sundry; there is no excuse. Either a dog is trained or he is not, there are no short cuts. If difference there be between the trial dog and the dog used purely for shooting it lies, not in the training, but in the trial dog's ability, his owner's expert training and, most important of all, in the vigilance exercised by his handler over the first two seasons whilst he is shooting over him. In short, a trial dog is a well trained, polished, shooting dog.

Take the time to train your dog properly and not only will he repay you a thousandfold, but there will be less likelihood of you paying the price for not doing the job properly by having a coronary attack.

CHAPTER ONE

The Very Beginning

CHOICE OF A PUPPY

I have yet to meet anyone who, with any degree of certainty, could select the best puppy in a litter at the tender age of 8 weeks old; personally I tend to leave this to my wife and her feminine intuition. Nevertheless, there are useful guidelines.

Let us imagine that you have answered an advertisement and are inspecting a litter of puppies around 8 weeks of age. Contrary to popular belief, the breeder does not know which is the best, for at this age they are just playful bundles of fun. A lot can happen and many changes take place between now and four months hence. The breeder in all probability will offer advice, but you must realise that he is just making an educated guess based on what he prefers and, as he is a different person from yourself, what may suit him may not suit you; therefore his 'guthunches', for this is about what they amount to, are of little use to you. Stories such as the first one out of the box, or the smallest in the litter because he has had to fight against his bigger brothers and sisters to get to the 'milk-bar', are common. Whilst I have never found any real evidence to support these theories, the one I like best, certainly the most feasible, is to lift all the puppies out of their box, and the one that the bitch carries back into the box first is your choice. The theory is of course, that that puppy is her favourite, and after all she should know best. But if you like a particular pup, then do not be swayed from your choice, for if you like it you will do well with it. Let your eye be your judge.

The questions you must ask yourself are:
1 Do you like the look of the puppies' surroundings, are they clean? If not, and if the breeder couldn't even bother to clean the kennel before you arrived, then what sort of an upbringing

have they had? I would under no circumstances buy from a filthy kennel.

2 Do they look healthy?

3 Are their legs straight?

4 Are they lively?

5 Are their tails docked properly, ie two-thirds left on?

Ask to see them outside and note their reactions both to the surroundings and to yourself. Look for a pup who bustles about. Even more important, look for a pup who watches you and climbs up your leg showing no nerves or fear. The colour or markings are of no consequence whatsoever, I believe that a good dog cannot be a bad colour. Ask permission to pick him up, look into his eyes. Are they well spaced? A dark-brown, rounded eye is a good eye. Never buy a puppy with a light or yellow one, this is known as a 'hard' eye. It should be a dark colour with a kindly look about it. The skull should be well rounded. If it is small, then you must ask yourself where does he keep his brains.

Once you have satisfied yourself on these points, ask to see the pedigree. Starting from the top left-hand corner, reading down, will be two names, sire and dam; these are the parents of your puppy. The next column, starting once again at the top of the page, are the grandparents; the next column, the great-grandparents, and so on. It is the first three generations which are the most important in the formation of your puppy's potential inherent qualities.

If on examination of these three generations you should see the initials SH/CH or show/bench winner, beside a particular dog or bitch's name, do not buy, for this means that there is show blood in the pedigree. The working and show blood should be kept separate, it is a shooting dog you require, not a brainless beauty. In my experience, in the vast majority of cases, show blood is harmful in a working dog's pedigree. Think about it for a moment. A show dog is bred through successive generations for improvement in looks, to win dog shows. Brains or hunting instincts do not play the slightest part in the motives of the breeders. They breed dogs to win cups at shows, in many cases with the ultimate aim of making profit, and by and large they would be horrified if you were to suggest that they use the occasional working dog in their breeding policy, for they know only too well that this would be harmful to the conformation of the progeny.

The working-dog enthusiast on the other hand, breeds his dogs for work with very little regard as to how they look – brains, hunting instinct, tractability, nose, mouth; these are his criteria, and of course they too breed and train for profit. Success in field trials increases the value, not only of the dog competing, but of his puppies as well. Thus field trials are the shop window of the shooting man. They maintain the standards to the ultimate betterment of the breed, from the working point of view.

There are always a few dedicated men and women who attempt to breed the dual purpose dog, ie the dog capable of winning shows and field trials. Whilst their motives are of the highest, I feel they are making a rod to break their own backs, for I have yet to see them succeed, certainly where the spaniel breed is concerned. Therefore if it is a working spaniel you require my advice to you must be, don't make life any more difficult than it is, buy from working parentage.

On examining the pedigree, you are looking for the initials F.T.CH. or F.T.W. which mean field trial champion and field trial winner. It is the generations of puppies descendent from these dogs that are bred for work. If there are two or three of these in the first three generations, or even more, and you like a particular puppy in the litter, then if the price is right – and at the time of writing the current price for quality is between £60 and £70 – go ahead and buy.

In the last few years however a disquieting situation has arisen with regard to pedigrees and the advertising of puppies for sale, and that is the misleading use of the letters F.T.W. It has become more and more obvious that, since the advent of field tests, an increasing number of participants are using these initials and confusing the public. A field test winner has only proved himself proficient in the most basic areas of training. As field tests are held in the summer months using dummies, a dog cannot be tried as regards mouth, nose or, in the case of a spaniel, for hunting; therefore such tests play little or no part in offering the public a yardstick by which to breed or purchase puppies. Anyone who knowingly uses these initials to confuse the customer into thinking that the dog is a field trial winner, is beneath contempt. Therefore, you would be well advised to ask the breeder if these letters F.T.W. indicate a field trial or a field test winner.

Another word of warning: if ultimately you envisage the possibility of running your dog or bitch in field trials, the puppy must be Kennel Club registrable. Therefore it is imperative at this stage to ascertain whether the parents are registered or not. If not, you could be on a sticky wicket. Both parents must be registered. In all probability, if you are dealing with a bona fide breeder, he will already have applied to the Kennel Club for the puppies to be registered.

It is common practice these days to purchase a puppy by telephone from an advertisement. I personally have reservations about this, prefering, when I am selling to see the client to form some opinion of him and of the type of home that the puppy is likely to go to. Nevertheless many puppies are sold in this manner, being delivered by rail in a travelling box. There is no need for anxiety as regards puppies travelling in this way, they tend to settle down fairly rapidly and sleep for the greater part of the journey. Furthermore British Rail staff are exceedingly conscientious with regard to livestock in their care. In all probability the breeder will not have fed the puppy before dispatch; this is to prevent the puppy being sick on the journey and does him no harm at all. Indeed, it is advantageous in that the puppy is welcomed into his strange new environment with the one thing that sets him at ease faster than any other – food.

It must be remembered, when buying a puppy over the 'phone, that you have entered into a verbal contract inasmuch as you have promised to send your cheque for the amount requested as soon as possible. Do not be dilatory in this respect, for this is a seller's market; quality puppies sell like the proverbial hot cakes. Furthermore the seller does not know you from Adam. It is truly surprising the number of people who will answer an advertisement, some of them many weeks after it appears, be very enthusiastic promising to send their cheque the very next morning, and are never heard of again. So do not blame the breeder if, through being late, your cheque is returned to you because your puppy has been sold to someone else.

Many buyers ask the breeder to keep the puppy for them for

a few weeks before collecting it. Should you through circumstances be forced to make this request, you must expect to pay for it. Puppies eat and demand a lot more time and attention than an adult dog, and the breeder has a living to make. All rail charges are your responsibility and are extra to the purchase price, these also must be included in your cheque. It is up to you to ascertain from the breeder what they are likely to be. He will probably have to enquire at the local station, thus several 'phone calls may be necessary before finalising the deal.

WHERE TO KEEP YOUR PUPPY

Before buying a puppy you will no doubt have decided where you are going to keep it. This depends on the individual's preference and circumstances. In my opinion, although the training will differ slightly – and this is catered for in this book – it makes little difference in the early days. Should you decide to integrate the puppy into family life, ie keep it indoors, then it will obviously have to be house trained. Furthermore the family will have to be educated as to how to handle a puppy, as there is no doubt that a great deal of problems in later life, especially in training, stem from the mishandling of the puppy in its formative months. Apart from behavioural problems that may be instilled from an early age, there is the very real danger of actual physical harm being inflicted on him; the most common being in the picking up and laying down.

It is surprising how few people know how to pick up a puppy correctly. When handling, it must always be borne in mind that he is just that, a puppy, consequently his bones are not yet properly formed. Most people tend to pick up with both hands around the rib cage, in this way the puppy's body weight is unevenly distributed, exerting strain on the internal organs, resulting very often in diaphragmatic hernia which can be fatal. The correct method of lifting a puppy is to pass one hand through between the rear legs, palm upwards, thus evenly supporting the full weight, whilst supporting the chin with the other hand.

Such problems of mishandling do not occur to such an extent if a puppy is kept out of doors in a kennel for most of the day. Indoors, surrounded by children, a puppy gets very little peace.

15

Throughout this book stress will constantly be laid on the importance of trying to understand what the dog is feeling and of taking into consideration the age, experience and by no means least the temperament, of both yourself and the dog. Therefore start as you mean to go on. Never, never, lose your temper with a dog. 'Act in haste and repent at leisure' might well have been coined with the training of dogs in mind.

It has never ceased to surprise me how a person who is perfectly rational in his or her role as a parent, when confronted with the simple task of getting the desired response from a dog, becomes irrational. Ask yourself this question, would you spank a baby of perhaps 6 months of age for soiling his nappy? Of course you wouldn't, then why hit a puppy for soiling on the floor? Unfortunately the dog has, in the unenlightened owner, inherited a hard task master. Many owners endow their canine companions with an intelligence far beyond the capabilities of any animal; they expect more from a dog than they do from their children. How often, have we heard, 'He understands every word we say?' What utter nonsense. Because his dog has, through habitually hearing a particular sound in association with a particular activity, place or time, responded to that sound, the owner imagines that his dog is of unusual intelligence.

A supreme example of human stupidity where a dog is concerned, was foisted on the television public a few months ago by that usually excellent show *That's Life* when Esther Rantzen interviewed the owner of the 'talking dog'. If it wasn't so pathetic it would be funny. The owner was pulling at the hair below the dog's chin as the dog made deep-seated growling noises in its throat, the undulating jaw movements made by the action of the owner's hands did the rest, and low and behold it actually sounded as though the dog was saying 'sausages'. How many millions of our gullible populace I wonder, believe to this day that they heard a talking dog. No doubt the interviewer treated it in a light-hearted vein, but obviously the owner didn't, and neither would the majority of the viewing public. For, like it or lump it, that is how we are in this country, and perhaps are even more so in America. It is this attitude which probably

1980 Kennel Club Champion Macsiccar Mint with his owner R. Knight.
A son of field trial winner Macsiccar Michele Mint also won the Tower
Bird Trophy for the spaniel under three years of age scoring the highest
number of points in field trials for the season 1978/79

The wrong way to support a puppy because it exerts strain on the internal organs

The correct way to support a puppy

forms the biggest stumbling block to the amateur trainer, he expects too much too soon.

Chastisement, except in the mildest degree such as a sharp rebuke in a gruff tone, should not be necessary at this tender age. If the puppy makes a puddle on the best carpet it is aggravating, but hold yourself in check for he knows no better, he is doing what comes naturally. If you strike him you will only frighten him and achieve nothing, except a bewildered puppy whose trust in you has been broken. There are many old wives' tales regarding this, the most common being to dip his nose in it. What that is supposed to convey to the dog is completely beyond me.

When the puppy soils or wets on the floor, catch him in the act. The best way to achieve this is to set aside two days when a responsible member of the family can be with the puppy, preferably in a room near a door leading outside. Members of the family may take the watching on a shift system. The important thing is that the puppy be observed all the time; you may read a book or watch television or some similar activity, but you must be watchful. Most of the day the puppy will sleep, but he will wake up at frequent intervals for periods of play. Immediately he awakes and you hear him or observe him stirring, be especially vigilant. Do not distract him, allow him to do his own thing; he will probably wander around, sniffing here and there. Be on your guard. As soon as you see him circling around at a particular spot take him gently by the scruff of the neck and, holding him firmly, drag him slowly, front paws slightly off the ground, to the outside door. Once outside, let him wander until he has completed the job. Immediately make a great fuss of him and take him back indoors. This must be repeated over and over again. Within a very short time a puppy of normal intelligence will understand your requirements and will indicate his by going to the door and squatting down or whining, scratching at the door etc. Once he has reached this stage you are almost home and dry, if you will excuse the pun.

When taking the puppy outside by this method, every effort must be made not to hurt or frighten him in any way. If you tend to be deficient in patience or to be bad-tempered, you must guard against this; much better in fact if you leave well

19

alone and let some other member of the family of a more placid temperament deal with this aspect of training.

Do not go away for long periods leaving a young puppy at home by himself. He is a baby and has to micturate frequently. Take him with you in the car if there is no alternative. Remember the sooner he becomes accustomed to the car the better the traveller he will become. I believe that many chronic bad travellers needn't have been, but were introduced to the car at too late an age. If you leave him at home, you must accept that he will make puddles and your housetraining régime could be in grave danger of total relapse. Should you arrive home to find a puddle on your carpet, the best way to remove the smell and prevent him from repeating the deed on that spot in the future, is to give the area a good squirt with a soda siphon.

A puppy left alone for long periods will become bored and chew, resulting very often in irreparable damage. Once again, there is no point in taking it out on him for he knows no better and, unless you catch him in the act, you have no hope of demonstrating just why he is getting punished. In these circumstances punishment is best left alone; after all it is your fault, not his.

When taking a puppy outside, it is a good idea to take him to the spot in which he last 'performed'. The scent will be strongest there and will act as an added inducement for him to get on with it, thus speeding up the whole episode.

A lively young puppy will want to investigate everything he finds; this is how he learns about the world around him. He will pick up objects and carry them around. Obviously you have articles which you don't wish damaged but, once again, keep cool. Gently remove the object from his mouth by squeezing his top gums with your thumb and forefinger, then give him an old sock or slipper to play with. It has your scent on it, and therefore he will accept it readily. On no account must anyone at any time chastise the puppy whilst he has something in his mouth. This is of paramount importance if confidence in retrieving in future training is to be achieved. Always give him the same object, he will soon look upon it as his own. Never, never, snatch objects from him, for by so doing you will encourage him to 'grip', thus hard mouth may be instilled.

Do not be surprised if he eats any food you leave lying around, for in this too he is only doing what comes naturally. Therefore once again there is no point in punishing him, for you will only confuse him. There is nothing to be gained by venting your anger on a dog for your own mistakes, or for that matter after the event. Always remember, if successful correction is to be achieved in any situation throughout a dog's life, he must be caught in the act, or at least within a minute or so of it, and dragged back to the spot in which he committed the crime, and chastised on that spot. In this way the dog will associate the deed with the correction.

A KENNEL DOG

It may be that you decide to keep your puppy out of doors in a kennel, full-time or for part of the day, for example whilst you are at work. A dog kept outside, away from the distractions of the family scene, is a far easier dog to train, inasmuch as he is more attentive to the person who allows him his freedom. However as with keeping a dog indoors, specific problems may arise, for instance if a dog is kept alone in a kennel. Possibly the best solution is to get the·best of both worlds by keeping him in a kennel, but bringing him indoors frequently to 'humanise' him. In this way you should be able to integrate him into the family and bring him up in such a way as to make him a bold and happy pup, wise in the ways of the world. At the same time you can keep a watchful eye on both the pup and the children, not to mention the wife.

A puppy brought away from the warmth and security of the litter and left alone in a kennel will be cold, frightened, and miss the company of his brothers and sisters. Thus in the dead of night he is liable to kick up the unholiest of rows, enough to awaken the dead. Exactly as in the case of a crying baby it is fatal to cater to this attention-seeking, for that is what it will develop into very quickly indeed, if you go out to him. If he sees that you will come when he calls, he will forever try it on. You must at all costs ignore him the first few nights, if you are to win in the end. Even the most persistent of puppies will get the message after the first couple of nights.

21

However, there are methods by which you may alleviate this problem to a certain degree. Beg, borrow, but get, an old stone hot-water bottle; fill it with hot water, roll it up in some stout sacking and stitch it in so that he cannot get into it and scald himself. In the dark he will use this as a substitute for the warmth of the litter. Its bulk and shape will be faintly reminiscent, in his tiny mind, of the shape and bulk of his mother's body and consequently will give him psychological security. Security will be enhanced if you procure an old clock which has a loud tick, and place it on a high shelf out of his reach. In my experience these methods have proved highly successful. In years gone by, before I was a professional, I lived in a tiny cottage on the perimeter of a large private housing estate, the inhabitants of which would get very narky indeed if my dogs so much as squeaked at night. On the arrival of every new puppy, I used the bottle and clock régime with great success.

At all times a puppy, or for that matter any dog, must have access to clean drinking water in ample quantities. This is even more important than food. He should be locked up at night and let out first thing in the morning. Spaniels, if encouraged to be so, are exceptionally clean-living dogs, and they soon adapt to a routine; thus by doing this you will save yourself a lot of kennel cleaning. Nevertheless, the kennel must be cleaned and disinfected regularly. A dog is not stupid, if you show him that you care for his well-being he will respect you for it.

The size of the kennel is dictated by individual choice and circumstances, but it must be of sound construction, waterproof, free from damp and draughts, and contain a timber sleeping-bench raised off the floor. Whether or not one uses straw in the bed is again entirely the individual's preference. I prefer not to, having found that straw or hay encourages skin vermin, and also encourages puppies to wet and soil their bed, causing more work for the owner. It is most desirable that a kennel should be warm in winter and cool in summer. This is easily achieved simply by lining the interior walls, ceiling and floor with fibre-glass matting such as roof insulation, readily available at any DIY shop. Obviously if a dog can get into this material and chew it, results would be disastrous to the dog's health, therefore the interior must be lined with a suitable wall boarding. This may

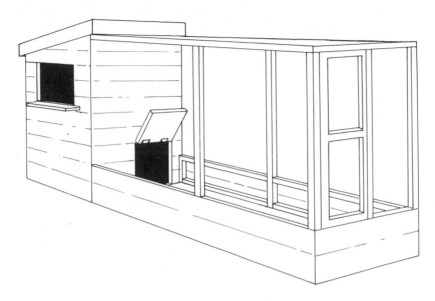

An ideal kennel and run

seem to be an unnecessary expense, but believe me it isn't. After a great deal of experience in building kennels, I have found that penny wise is most definitely pound foolish; skimp, and I can assure you you will regret it.

It is essential for cleaning purposes that there be a normal-sized door leading into the kennel, and a smaller door approximately 15in × 12in for the dog to gain access to his run. A longish run is better than a square one, for it encourages the dog to run up and down. I have found the ideal size to be 12–18ft × 5ft. Grass runs are of no earthly use whatsoever; apart from the obvious risk of the dog digging his way out, they can be the very devil to keep clean. Flagging stones cemented between the joints is as good as anything, cement alone tends to be damp and encourages rheumatism. I have heard that if cinders are mixed with the cement this alleviates this problem but, never having tried it, I cannot recommend it. For hygienic reasons it is essential that the run should slope down from the kennel to the front of the run, preferably into a drain.

Dogs are born escapologists, and I have never owned a dog that could not get through chicken-wire like the proverbial hot knife through butter. Therefore, if you are to spare yourself much hard work and heartbreak, do the run-making job thoroughly at the outset, it's cheaper in the end. The ideal material is galvanised weld-mesh of 2 × 2 × 12 gauge. Fixed at suitable intervals to 2in × 2in creosoted timber on the inward-facing planes, this will afford an efficient stockade. The 'walls' of the run should be approximately 8ft high and turned inward at the top to prevent the dog jumping or climbing out.

FEEDING YOUR PUPPY OR DOG

An 8 week old puppy (see also Chapter 14) requires at least four meals per day, gradually decreasing in number and increasing in quantity to two meals per day at 7 to 8 months old. On and after this, for the rest of the dog's life, I feed him twice a day – a light milky breakfast with a few dog biscuits or cereal first thing in the morning, with the main meal at night, after exercise. Never feed a dog a heavy meal before exercise, or for that matter a journey in a car. I have always held the view that during the intensive working periods of a dog's life, he should be fed like a navvy if he is to be expected to work like one. A half-starved dog cannot possibly give of his best. A puppy should be slightly plump, without being fat and flabby. Too much cow's milk is a bad thing because the water volume in it is too great for a puppy's kidneys to cope with, so not too much milk. An adult dog should be fed six days per week and fasted on the seventh, when only clean, fresh drinking water should be available to him. This prevents his system from becoming sluggish and to a small degree helps his coat.

There is no doubt in my mind that when there is only one dog, there is an ample supply of kitchen scraps with which to satisfy his needs. Nevertheless, this needs enlarging on to prevent misunderstanding. By kitchen scraps I do not mean rubbish, but scraps from the dinner table, excluding bacon rind, potatoes, white bread or starch, of any kind.

For the sake of convenience tinned food may be given, so long as it is mixed with a good-quality dog biscuit; it must never be fed on its own. Just as we like variety, so does a dog. Of course your dog will eat it, and no doubt appear to relish it; so would you if you were given nothing else. Like us, a dog requires a well-balanced diet containing adequate proportions of protein, carbohydrate and fats. The addition of finely chopped green vegetables, preferably raw, is an excellent source of vitamins and minerals.

SUGGESTED DIET GUIDE

For Carbohydrate Content
Brown toasted bread
Good quality dog biscuits
Brown dog rusks
These can be soaked in gravy, milk, raw egg, or soup.

For Protein Content
Boiled or steamed fish (if you can afford it)
Egg (raw) or boiled and finely chopped
Good quality (all-in-one) dog meal, but not too often.
Meat (lean). Rabbit boiled in its fur and the bones removed is
    first-class. Sheeps' heads are excellent, provided they are
    thoroughly cooked (your butcher will skin them and split them
    for you). Feed all 'the meat including the brains and eyes.
Best of all is raw green tripe (unwashed) if you can get it, and if
    you can stand the stench.

Minerals and Additives
Whatever diet you choose, the following minerals and additives should be included regularly:

Adexoline (5 drops per day). This contains the A, D and C vitamins. If your puppy tends to have rickety legs this will help to straighten them. Available at any chemist.

Vetsymes or Canovel tablets (5 per day). This gives B vitamins.

Everfree ($\frac{1}{2}$ teaspoonful for every 10lb of body weight). If administered daily, this will not only keep your dog free from intestinal parasites for the rest of his life, but provide a valuable mineral source. Available from most good pet shops.

There are many all-in-one dog foods on the market which provide an alternative form of feeding. They provide an easy to handle, complete balanced diet as long as they are fed according to the manufacturers' instructions. Nevertheless, I have never come across one that would put flesh on a thin dog.

SUMMARY

1 Remember at all times he is a baby, do not expect too much too soon.
2 A dog is conditioned into reacting in a certain way to a certain sound. Whether it be voice, whistle, clicking the tongue, or any sound. If that sound is used consistently with a certain activity, together with demonstration of what is required in gradual stages, then by degrees a conditioned response will be obtained.
3 Physical chastisement will only result in making the puppy distrust you, maintain a rapport by conditioning the puppy in the play situation.
4 Do not feed a puppy, or an adult dog for that matter, before a journey in a car. He will throw up.
5 Never snatch objects out of his mouth for this will teach him to grip.
6 Never chastise him, frighten him by shouting at him or chase him when he has something in his mouth. Intercept him by all means, but don't chase him, and once you have him stroke him gently and soothe him as you remove it.
7 Remember, a dog associates the deed with the spot in which he committed it.

CHAPTER TWO

The Puppy up to 6 Months Old

DEVELOPMENT

The first few months of a dog's life are equivalent to the formative years in a child's life and are, therefore, very important. It is during these formative months that the foundation of your dog's future personality is laid and consequently they have a great influence on his success or failure in training, and his ultimate performance in the shooting situation. Therefore, at the very outset it is of vital importance that you understand how a dog thinks.

First and foremost, he does not understand every word you say, or anything like it. A very intelligent dog, over a long period of time, will associate certain sounds with specific activities, and in due course will build up a memory bank of perhaps fifteen to twenty sounds.

Another important point which I suspect the majority of dog trainers both amateur and professional fail to take into account is that a dog's field of vision is very different from ours. His eye-level is much lower, consequently his horizons are much nearer. Very often I have observed a dog mark a bird down and, on being sent for it, go rocketing out and start hunting for it perhaps twenty to thirty feet short of the fall. This is very common on rising ground (see over) and, though a small point, is well worth remembering. In such a situation, a young inexperienced dog will quickly become confused, and if the bird is a runner it will very soon be 'out of the parish' and unpickable.

WHEN AND HOW TO PUNISH

The most important thing to remember at all times when handling a dog, whether as a puppy being trained or later in

A dog's horizon is very different from ours

the shooting field, is that he associates his deeds with the spot in which he commits them. In other words, if a dog disobeys you at point A there is no point in catching him at point B and punishing him, for he will think that he is being punished for the last thing he did, ie at point B. Reams and reams of paper have been used by countless writers in trying to get this simple but very important point across to the shooting public, and yet we see numerous examples every shooting season which clearly indicate that it still is not understood. Understand and implement this one lesson with consistency, and training a dog is at least 50 per cent simpler.

Possibly the confusion arises in the way in which the problem has sometimes been explained. Generally speaking, what happens seems to be this. The book is read and the trainer, realising that this rule is an important facet of training, makes up his mind that he will apply it. Sooner or later the situation arises that necessitates swift action, but as these crises rarely occur when expected, the poor trainer is caught on the hop, the little devil has done the deed and is now either careering off into the next parish or is engrossed in some other activity. What is to be done for, taking the book literally, the dog is now at point B, C or D, and therefore it is too late to punish him.

The answer is very simple, walk up to the dog quietly, command him to drop, quietly. Don't make a great noise about it, you are not punishing the dog – yet, and you do not want to instill the idea that you are at this point. Take the dog by the scruff of the neck, don't speak to him at all, drag him back to the exact spot in which the crime was committed, and administer the correction there.

This can be very hard work, nevertheless you must be pedantic about this. A dog must never best you, for dogs are supreme optimists and should they best you once by getting away with it, they will forever and a day try it on.

A dog is very basically a pack animal and his instincts are such. He must at all times know his place in the pack, and in this instance the pack consists of you and he. This pack instinct is much stronger in the male of the species, which is why some people have much more difficulty in training a dog as opposed to a bitch, the bitch's role in the pack being one of subservience to the male. Her challenging 'instincts' therefore are not as strong as those of the male in the training situation. You, at all times must be the dominant partner, the pack leader. How masculine or feminine a dog's personality is dictates the extent to which he or she will try you on. Some dogs never do, others will, consistently. It is, therefore, of utmost importance that over the first few months of your puppy's life you assess his personality correctly and treat him accordingly.

By this I do not wish to give the impression that because a dog is 'hard' you must be unkind to him to achieve success, nothing could be further from the truth. But, in the case of the hard dog, more vigilance is required to prevent him from developing bad habits. In the majority of cases the wild uncontrollable dog, is the end result of careless training and/or handling – bad habits are instilled, a bad dog is yet to be born. Granted, through bad breeding a dog may have inherent faults, but provided the breeding is good so that no inherent faults are present, he has the necessary qualities. It is for the breeder, through developing the puppy correctly and by judicious training, to mould those qualities to his or her requirements.

Very often a young puppy who charges about with great enthusiasm is mistakenly thought of as 'hard', when in fact he is not. Do not be too quick at assessing him. He may well be quite sensitive beneath this boisterous image which you should be pleased to see, for it proves that he has confidence in your company. It is this panache for living that we wish to foster and ultimately mould to our advantage.

Remember, each dog is different, just as we are, they are individuals. Consequently the training, although fundamentally the same, differs from dog to dog, according to the environment and to the personality of both dog and trainer. It is this ability to adapt from dog to dog that differentiates between the good trainer and the bad. If you assess your puppy wrongly you are beaten before you start, for if he is a bold customer he will grow and ultimately train you. On the other hand if he is of a sensitive disposition and you employ tactics which frighten him, he may never build up his confidence in you again.

However, without exception, the secret of success in training is the avoidance of the dangerous situation. Never let the dog see the rabbit until he is well and truly steady to the drop whistle. It is as simple as that; skimp, and you will without doubt live to regret it.

You must take your time in the early stages of getting to know your puppy; observe his reactions to every conceivable situation, to strange objects, to people, then form your own opinion. Be sure that you are correct before embarking on the training proper. As you will not commence serious training until the puppy is at least 6 months old, you have plenty of time.

Under no circumstances must you begin training before then, and although in this chapter I may appear to be telling you to train your puppy in certain things, I am not. We are developing the puppy in the play situation for what is yet to come. If you overdo these activities you are training. You must not draw the puppy's attention to these exercises by making a big thing out of them. Their whole object is to form good habits as opposed to bad, so that ultimately you have a cornerstone upon which to build. Thus, this chapter is the most important in the book, for it is the foundation of all training yet to come.

Before you chastise a dog, be sure at all times that he knows why he is being punished. In other words never punish a dog for committing a crime until he has been well and truly shown in earlier training what is, or is not, required of him in this particular respect. He learns by example and association, ie experience; thus you do not punish a dog if he is still just a puppy for chasing a rabbit, for he has not been trained not to. In a very young puppy, chastisement should never exceed taking him by the scruff of the neck to the spot where he has misbehaved and shaking him (plate, p. xx).

Whilst I may appear to have dwelt on this question of chastisement at some length, I have done so to emphasise its importance. I want you to read this over and over again until you understand fully what I am saying. Far better that you avoid a potentially dangerous situation than tempt providence and regret it. Do not get into a situation which might encourage the dog to do wrong, and thus avoid the necessity of punishing him. This applies throughout the training. It allows you to remain on good terms with the dog, it is the positive approach rather than the negative. Always play safe.

DEVELOPING OBEDIENCE

From the very outset, start as you mean to go on. If you give a command that you know the puppy understands and has complied with in the past, insist on it. Herein lies a very common danger, however – far too many owners nag their dog. Do not give unnecessary commands just for the sake of it, or to show your visitors just how good your puppy is, for sooner or later he will get so sick of listening to you that he will simply switch off and ignore you. Command only when necessary.

Very often people call at my kennels with puppies that they are training. Most of these puppies are far too advanced for their age, old before their time. Very often after a long journey of perhaps a hundred miles or so the owner, no doubt in an effort to impress me, will get the puppy out of the car and immediately command it to sit, only to be extremely upset and puzzled when the puppy will not do so. I would doubt a dog's intelligence if he did; he is excited at getting out of the car, probably his first thought is a call of nature, so why make life difficult.

It is this inability to relax over training that causes many problems for the amateur. Most of these puppies have problems instilled in them by their owners' eagerness to press on to more interesting exercises. It is not unusual for an owner to expound enthusiastically on how his puppy of 6 or 7 months of age can go out each evening for an hour to quarter its ground, turn on a whistle, drop to a whistle and come back to a whistle, sit and stay at distance to a hand-signal, plus retrieve to hand fur or feather. I have been met with a surprised look when on occasions I have asked them if they thought their children of perhaps 8 years or a little older should not be at university. For if you think about it they are expecting the equivalent from their puppy.

If a puppy of approximately 6 months of age will sit to a hand-signal and retrieve a dummy to hand plus return to a whistle whilst it is scampering about, then I am satisfied, that is quite sufficient. Just as with your children, a puppy must have his childhood, he must develop in an environment of control tempered with good-natured understanding.

As I have said, the majority of problems which arise in training are due to a fault in the trainer, not the dog. We are all guilty of thinking that our dog is better than he is, and to a greater or lesser degree are blind to his faults. You must guard against this. Some trainers tend to be too soft with a bold out-going dog, whilst others are too hard on a soft or sensitive animal; therefore, you must be honest with yourself, try not to cloud your judgement with sentiment. Always be firm but fair. For instance if on being told to kennel your puppy is reluctant to go in, take him gently by the scruff of the neck and drag him gently but firmly into the kennel, repeating 'Kennel' in a firm voice. Don't pick him up and throw him in as I have seen done by trainers who should know better.

Each day upon giving him his meals, hold the dish in your left hand (if you are right-handed) and, raising the right hand with palm held flat outwards, say, 'Hup' in a clear firm voice. The first few times you do this the puppy will jump around and generally play the fool, eventually sitting down to contemplate the situation for a second. Immediately his bottom touches the ground, put the dish of food down in front of him. It is truly amazing how rapidly a puppy can cotton on to what is required of him and in a very short time will, upon seeing the hand raised in this manner, sit immediately. As time goes on you can lengthen the time that he has to sit before the food is placed in front of him. Some authorities advocate teaching the puppy to wait until told to eat it; as I can see no valid reason for this added refinement, I do not bother.

Try not to leave a young puppy alone in a kennel for long periods. Talk to him in passing, go to him now and again, even if it is only to talk to him and fuss him for a few seconds. On leaving the kennel, always say, 'Kennel, good boy, kennel'. Take him out for short periods, frequently. In this way your puppy will not fret. A puppy left alone in a kennel for long periods will mature very slowly. Bear in mind it is of no importance to the puppy who feeds him so long as he gets food. But the person who gives him his freedom is, in his eyes, the master; it is to this person he will give his allegiance. Don't overdo the exercise periods, for he will tire easily, 10 minutes is enough. In any training session at this stage, little and often is the golden rule. When out with him, play with him, relax, get him to love you, let him scamper about. This is how he builds his muscles and learns about the world around him.

It is advisable early in a puppy's life to introduce him to the lead. However, at this stage of the game, you must not be too severe with him. The object of this exercise is purely and simply to get him used to the feel of something around his neck. You must not frighten him or he will have unpleasant associations regarding the lead.

You must not teach a puppy to walk to heel at this stage, walking to heel is one of the very last things that you teach a hunting dog. More puppies than I would care to count have been brought in to me for training because, through being taught to walk to heel too early in their lives, they were reluctant to hunt out in front. I suspect that in many instances the owners have been listening to the field-test pundits, for since the advent of the field test this has become an all too common complaint. If you think about it, it's only common sense, for if you implant in a young dog's mind that he walks at your heel and then ask him to 'Get on' or 'Hi – seek', you are presenting him with a contradiction, you are confusing him. Believe me there are enough contradictions in the training of dogs without manufacturing any more. A spaniel above all things must be a hunter, so when he's a puppy keep him full of bounce, happy and active.

Now, back to the lead. I want you to put it (slip type, not a choke chain, as this tends to bind and choke a young dog) on your puppy when he is out with you, preferably after he has had a runabout and just for short periods, initially. These periods can be lengthened as the weeks go by. The first time he will probably resent this restriction on his liberty and will pull, twist, roll on his back, get between your legs, and generally react like a fish on the end of a line. You must exercise tolerance here; patience, and all will come right in the end. If you choose an open space to work in, you can more or less avoid the tangle and go with him, at the same time letting him feel a little pressure. On each subsequent period on the lead he will by degrees react less and less, until he is quite familiar to this restriction to his liberty and is calm. He can then be walked on the lead for some distance.

Once he has attained this standard you will note that the puppy will begin to pull on the lead to his obvious discomfort. This is undesirable, both from your point of view and his. The remedy is quite simple, whenever he gets to the full extent of the lead give him a short sharp tug. Never let this exercise develop into a tug-of-war, a long hard pull on the lead is quite useless; short and sharp at all times, he will soon learn. It must be understood, however, that in the case of a hunting dog you are not training him to walk to heel, just to walk comfortably at your side. If you keep cool, the end result will be achieved in the minimum of time.

During these short exercise periods, occasionally call the puppy up to you by name, at the same time encouraging him by crouching down to welcome him. He will come scampering back to you quite readily at this age, for it is all a game to him, and we want to keep it a game for as long as possible. Do not overdo any aspect of training at any time in a dog's life, for therein lies the problem of boredom which encourages disobedience, thus necessitating punishment. The secret in training dogs is never to place yourself in a position where you issue commands that you cannot possibly enforce.

As soon as you see that the puppy is keen to scamper back to you, introduce him to a whistle; a small one with a high pitch is ideal. Do not train a dog to the silent type of whistle, for a

Another correct way of picking up a puppy

House training: drag him slowly, front paws slightly off the ground, to the outside door

very good reason. This whistle has a tone regulator, thus the tone is variable, probably quite undetectable to our ears but certainly not to the dog's. I like to hear the tone and pitch of the whistles I use; the small black buffalo horn or the plastic equivalent are ideal. Some of these have a pea inside but my advice is to remove it, for later you will be incorporating a thunderer whistle in the training solely to drop the dog, and we do not want to encourage confusion between the two whistles.

When you call your puppy up to you as he is scampering about, in addition to the vocal command, crouch down and give two small peeps on the whistle. To encourage a smart response, all whistle signals throughout a dog's training must be short and sharp; elongated whistle commands encourage a sloppy, listless reaction. Your puppy will, within a few days, be coming to the whistle alone.

Praise is of paramount importance at this stage. The puppy must learn to associate coming back to you with a feeling of pleasure. Never scold him when he is on his way back, the idea of course being to eventually get him to be bold and confident in his return to you. If a dog is dilatory about coming back, there is not much chance of him ever delivering a retrieve to hand; only common sense after all, isn't it?

Keep the puppy bold and happy, right up to at least 6 months old. Don't rush on to training proper, for then you are attempting to put an old head on young shoulders. Remember at all times that he's just a baby; treat him as such, make allowances.

LEARNING TO RETRIEVE

Now we come to a really sticky aspect – retrieving. Probably there are more problems with this than any other sphere of training, and most are instilled in one way or another by the owner or his family. First there are the children who, whilst daddy is at work, will amuse themselves by unendingly throwing uninteresting objects for the puppy to bring back. The obvious danger here is twofold, either they will sicken the puppy so much that he will ultimately refuse to pick up, or by pulling and snatching objects out of his mouth they will encourage him to

37

grip. So warn the kids that they are not to throw things for him, nor have they to chase him around the garden, for herein lies another very common problem. Whilst you in your spare time are trying to encourage the puppy to come to you, the children are busy illustrating to the puppy the joys of being chased. You can then hardly blame the pup if one evening, on being called up to you, he decides it would be much more fun if you were to chase him.

Wives also, if not enlightened, can be a bit of a disturbing element in this respect. If the puppy is kept in the house, you must try and understand her position. The little devil will get into everything, pick up and run around with objects whilst her back is turned. He has no sense of value, so will chew anything that takes his fancy. Your wife, who is probably busy with a thousand and one chores around the house, has no time to exercise canine psychology, so her natural reaction is to snatch the blasted thing out of his mouth after she has chased him upstairs and downstairs etc. From the puppy's point of view this is great fun, but not so if he plays the wife up to such an extent that she loses her temper and belts him one. Such are the trials and tribulations of keeping a puppy in the house, so be warned.

Obviously we have to prepare the puppy for future training in the art of retrieving; a gun dog that will not retrieve, after all is said and done, isn't worth a light. So, taking the puppy alone out of his kennel to an area where there are no distractions, allow him to scamper about. As soon as he is on the move, whilst he is still fresh and full of go, throw a small soft dummy a short distance out in front of him – a sock rolled up is ideal for this for it has a scent to it. It is important that you make this easy for him, let him see you make the throw. He will scamper out eagerly for the dummy, however, do not expect him to come rushing back to you with it, for his most likely reaction will be to pick it up and go careering off. Do not alarm him by shouting or 'losing your cool'. Give him his two peeps on the whistle, repeat this if necessary, and at the same time crouch down. In nine cases out of ten he will come running up to you, when you will be able to hold him and fondle him for a few moments before removing the dummy gently from his mouth. Should it be apparent that after your crouching down and uttering the

38

whistle signal he is more intent in shaking and playing with the object than he is in you, swift unflappable action is required. Get up from your crouching position, attract his attention, and run off slowly in the opposite direction. The object is not to run away from him, but to get him to think you are, at the same time letting him catch you. As soon as he does, give him exaggerated praise.

Once again I must emphasise that at this stage you are not training, it is a game. Make a big thing of it and you are trying to train him, but he is still too young. We are at this stage laying the foundations, preparing the way for what is to come. This 'exercise', for want of a better name, must on no account be overdone. One mini-retrieve per exercise period is more than sufficient. Indeed if I were to say one per every other session, I would not be playing oversafe. Yet I can hardly blame the amateur trainer for overdoing this when I read a book recently wherein the author advocates giving a puppy multiple retrieves along a corridor every day – what utter nonsense. Still the general public are not to know that. After all one assumes, and I think it is a fair assumption, that if someone writes a specialised book, they must be an authority on the subject. Alas such is not necessarily the case.

It is important that when the puppy returns to you with the object, you show him first and foremost that you are pleased with him, whilst he still has the object in his mouth. After praising him, you gently remove it. A few puppies will give up their prize quite readily, but the majority are reluctant for the first few times and require a little gentle persuasion. As outlined in Chapter 1, gently squeeze the gums.

By your demeanour the puppy must be encouraged to think of these little interludes in his daily routine as pleasurably as possible. The ease with which he adapts to 'delivering the goods' depends on his temperament and age when these 'exercises' are first introduced into his curriculum. Obviously if you have bought a pup of around 6 months old straight out of a kennel, who has not been introduced to carrying, you may find a little more difficulty than you would with a puppy of half that age.

One of the commonest problems concerns the puppy who, perhaps due to anxiety in relation to coming back, eye-shyness

39

(a lot more common than most people realise), or a traumatic experience, has associated coming back to you with distrust. He will come so far back and then either try to rush past you, or circle around just out of reach. Whilst this is very aggravating, rather than lose your temper you would be better advised to curtail the exercise, go home with the puppy in a good frame of mind, sit down and think things out. Do not act in haste. Ask yourself 'why?' – there must always be a reason. Can you recall having done something which may have a bearing on the pup's behaviour? It is probably something very simple, so simple that you cannot see the wood for the trees as in the following example.

Recently I changed my glasses for the new-type bifocals with photochromic lenses. I was quite puzzled to find that during the next few days even my most seasoned field-trial dogs would not, or were at the very least reluctant to, deliver to hand. Luckily I was being photographed for one of my articles in *Sporting Gun* a few days later and, on seeing the proofs, noticed that where my eyes usually were, there were two great black orbs. The problem was solved. These glasses obviously were inducing a type of eye-shyness in the dogs. But as usual, if the cause is known, the solution is simple – in this particular instance, the same cure as in normal cases of eye-shyness, ie avert the eyes as the dog approaches, was followed.

If you come to the conclusion that your puppy is trying to get past you or circling because of anxiety, you must illustrate by example that, far from anything to fear he will be rewarded, in this case by praise when he comes into hand. The immediate solution of course is to make it more difficult for the puppy either to get past or indulge in circling around you. Therefore stand with your back against a wall when you throw the dummy, crouch down, encourage him in with voice, whistle, clapping your hands etc, anything you can think of, but be calm, do not, by getting uptight, draw his attention to the fact that anything is amiss.

If at first you don't succeed, call it a day, make a big thing of playing with the puppy on your way home. Try letting him run around and test him with the recall whistle. If he now comes in readily to hand, your problem is obviously related to the

40

actual retrieving, so you must think about the type of dummy you are using and try various objects. Experimentation may be your key to success. As already mentioned, if for one reason or another a dog will not come back to you naturally, without fear, you have little chance of success in getting him to come into hand with something in his mouth.

If when you throw a dummy, your puppy runs out, touches it, or sniffs at it, then walks off unconcernedly, you really have got problems, for this is the classic symptom of an inherently reluctant retriever, and at very least the sign of a puppy that has been sickened in relation to picking up. The first case may prove very difficult to eradicate but, by experimentation, a cure may be found; the second alternative may prove well-nigh impossible to cure. It depends on the degree of abreaction in the puppy. In both cases, after due consideration, one usually comes to what is after all the obvious conclusion, that as the puppy is not interested in that particular 'retrieve', a more interesting object must be utilised. Very often the most unlikely objects can turn a dog on in this respect; only experimentation will offer a solution.

Here I would like to say a word about what is known in the trade as 'force-retrieving'. This is an aspect of training that I would, under no circumstances, advocate. Firstly there most definitely is an element of cruelty involved, secondly the chances of success are extremely remote, thirdly it seems to me that if a dog has to be forced to retrieve he is not worth the trouble. He has a very serious fault, and is therefore not worth spending money on. There are some authorities who would not agree with this, indeed who actually force-retrieve their puppies whether they need it or not. But this begs the question. If the puppy is a natural carrier, why embark upon a régime which is risky in the extreme, and which at best will achieve very little, if anything at all. For if the puppy is a natural, it will do nothing to enhance his capabilities; on the other hand if it is unsuccessful, it may put the puppy off retrieving for life. When one considers that even in skilled professional hands the ratio of success is very low, it is certain that as far as the amateur at least is concerned this is an area of training best left well alone.

It is desirable at this stage to encourage the puppy to get

41

over or under obstacles; therefore if when out with him you encounter a simple obstacle such as a wire fence, gate etc, providing there is a way under, climb over, at the same time saying, 'Over, over, good dog, over'. We know a small puppy is not going to sprout wings and fly over a gigantic obstacle, but he will work his way through or under. That is all we want at this point – we are preparing the way for what is yet to come by instilling an association between the sound 'over' and his overcoming the obstacle. We also want to lay the foundations of independence consequently, providing there is a way through or under, once you have surmounted the obstacle walk on slowly and encourage him through. But do not help him physically; he must learn this one by himself.

Once again different puppies react in widely different ways. Don't be alarmed at the caterwauling that may go on, just keep increasing the distance between you slowly, encouraging him all the time vocally. It must be realised that a young puppy has not fully developed his eyesight, and some puppies have difficulty in focusing on a distant object, so make allowances. You may get as far away as 30–40yd and the puppy really gets into a panic. As this is unnecessary and you do not wish to prolong it, walk quickly back calling him by name, wave an arm to help him re-focus on you, then start all over again.

Remember that a dog's eyesight is different from ours. Not only are his horizons lower, but I suspect that eyesight is the least developed sense the dog possesses, his nose and ears being much more important. However, this varies tremendously from dog to dog. If, later in life when hunting in woodland on a dull winter day you give him a whistle signal, you may see him stop, look around for, even straight at you, and yet quite obviously not be focusing on you. On repetition of the signal he may go charging off in the wrong direction altogether. In my opinion, this is a combination of echo and his reluctance to believe his eyes, depending more on his senses – nose and ears – in that order. When out shooting, our clothes do tend to be on the drab side and merge, as they are intended to do, with the surroundings.

It is a common sight to see a dog come back to a line of 'guns' and work his way down the line to his owner. This is because he has lost the place, he has got disorientated momentarily and will even come very close to some in the line to 'wind' them. I remember a shepherd telling me, many years ago, that he could recognise each individual sheep by its face. This was completely beyond me and at the time I thought he was pulling my leg, even to this day I could scrutinise closely half a dozen sheep and they would all look alike to me. Likewise, to many dogs, one man in a Solway zipper looks very much the same as another in the same garb. In field trials I always wear the same orange towelling scarf for this very reason, and have found that it helps the dog to focus on me and make a speedy delivery – there are tricks in all trades. If you wish to test this theory, and supposing that you are in the habit of wearing a particular mode of dress when taking the dog out, change it completely in style and colour one day and approach his kennel from some way off. Many dogs will treat you as a complete stranger, some right up to sniffing you. Bear these things in mind, it all helps to understand a dog's psychology.

HUMANISING

At 12–16 weeks old it is desirable to have the puppy injected against leptospirosis and distemper. Your local vet will do this for you, but be sure to get a certificate from him saying that this has been done, together with the date and brand name of injection used. Keep this certificate in a safe place, it will help the vet when you wish him to give the puppy a booster.

Up to this age the puppy will have an immunity to these diseases from the antibodies from his mother's milk. However, from any time after approximately 12 weeks of age this immunity will wear off, and from then on the puppy will be vulnerable. And the puppy who, for one reason or another, has never suckled at his mother's teats and has had to be brought up on the bottle, has no immunity to these diseases.

After he has been immunised you may take your puppy anywhere. However, bear in mind that some vets give two injections within a fortnight of one another; it depends on the brand of vaccine used. In this case you have to be doubly careful between the first and second injection not to allow your puppy to run on ground where other dogs have been. Once the puppy has been injected it is advisable to take him out continually to different places. He will learn about the world around him in this way. Let him meet people, run around on rough grass and in light bracken. Let him investigate anything – under your supervision of course – which takes his fancy.

If he dwells on certain spots say, 'Leave it', in a firm low voice and walk slowly on, repeating your command if necessary. Teaching him this command will be an invaluable aid in the future when out hunting, and it is really quite amazing how quickly a puppy can pick up its meaning. At this age, too, it is as well to teach him the word 'no', which can be incorporated with the above command as well as being used on its own. These two commands are the most important sounds in a dog's life.

Never let a dog run riot on his own or in the company of other dogs. Beware of fields containing livestock. Not only will a farmer take a dim view if he sees you wandering uninvited on his land, but a herd of young bullocks will give your puppy and you something to think about if they catch sight of you. Dogs who chase sheep deserve anything they get. Don't blame the farmer if he shoots your dog, he is entitled to, the blame is yours. Bear in mind always that whether you are with the dog or not, you are responsible for him and liable for damages resulting from his actions. It is advisable to take out an insurance against this. The Canine Defence League, or your local insurance broker, can furnish you with addresses.

Between 3 and 6 months old there is no real harm done if your puppy should stumble across a rabbit in his 'seat' and give chase; however I most strongly advise against making a habit of it. Should he chase, let him. Do not make a great noise about it, do not chase after him and punish him. Too many young puppies are put off hunting for life because of this, or at best inhibited. Indeed I have on occasions had spaniels brought into me for training who were actually frightened of scent. And, before anybody rolls about in the aisles laughing, let me enlarge upon this.

We go back to how a dog thinks. He learns by association, therefore let us imagine that a 3 month old puppy has just found a rabbit in its 'seat'. His owner, because of anxiety about future training, ie the steadiness of the puppy, jumps on him and gives him a hiding because he chased a rabbit. A few days later the puppy finds another rabbit; the owner gives him another hiding. Naturally the puppy is not too happy about this, and begins to think. Later on he begins to scent another rabbit, moves up tentatively towards it and, as he finds the rabbit, there is a great roar from the owner and the thunderous sound of feet charging towards him. The puppy's natural reaction is to run out of the way of the approaching danger, ie the owner. He does just that – he takes evasive action. The owner jumps on him, eventually catches him and gives him another hiding. Very soon indeed the puppy will associate the scent with the rabbit and the consequent hiding and in a very short time, on encountering this scent of the rabbit, will come running back to your feet. There you have it, the embryonic stage of a dog refusing to hunt because he has been conditioned. I believe it is quite possible to abreact (or condition) a dog to almost anything, whether sight, smell or sound. Never forget that a spaniel above all things must be a hunter so, if he does find a rabbit and chase it, do not draw his attention to it by shouting or losing your temper. The question of steadiness will be dealt with in good time when he is ready for it. For the time being, when you see him returning from the chase, give him the return signal with your whistle, and on his arrival take the opportunity of praising him for returning to you as opposed to punishing him for running away. Thus not only will you be forearmed regarding his education on ground game in the future, but your puppy will be unaware that he has bested you. That is of paramount importance.

I make a practice of walking over the ground I intend running the dog on with an old campaigner who clears the rabbits off for me. I then return to the car and take the puppy to the ground alone, leaving the older dog in the car. He has fulfilled his function by clearing the ground. A point to note here, however, is that if your older dog is prone to chase, you should position your car on the road so that the puppy cannot view the proceedings.

The benefit is obvious. Here I have a piece of ground with no game on it, but which contains scent to get the pup's nose down and him bustling around without temptation being put in his way – the dangerous situation has been avoided. You can never put too much scent up a puppy's nostrils if you do it this way. If you do not possess an older dog, walk the ground yourself, poking at all likely 'seats' with a stick.

Letting the puppy meet people has been mentioned. There is a very good reason for this; it will give him confidence in their company. Let them make a fuss of him, this will do no harm. Never mind the old wives' tale, 'Don't pat a working dog' – this is nonsense. When an owner says this, it is basically because he feels insecure about his own capabilities of training the dog. A working dog can soak up love like a sponge, providing you show him that when you give a command it must be obeyed.

You should educate the family, especially the children. Children, because they play, can be of invaluable assistance in humanising a puppy, if they are enlightened. At this stage there is no harm done if the wife takes him into the house, but the puppy must not be treated as a fool. Do not teach him tricks like begging for titbits. I at no time give chocolates or sweets to a dog; I have been known to bribe a dog in order to achieve a particular result, however only as a last resort.

EQUIPMENT FOR TRAINING A GUN DOG

The equipment mentioned up to this point is quite sufficient until the dog is 6 months old. But now is the appropriate time to include a list of equipment needed for the entire training of a gun dog. Although not required for the early education of the puppy, it will be needed from now on.

1 set of whistles, ie, 1 thunderer and 1 single pitch
1 small canvas dummy (home-made) 3in × 3in filled with sawdust
2 fur dummies (rabbit skins nailed to a small log 6in × 2in are ideal)
1 feather dummy (duck and pheasant wings tied together)
1 .22 blank starter pistol (some people use a toy cap pistol; this is quite permissible and much cheaper)

If you wish you may procure a dummy launcher. Used sensibly, this can be a very useful and versatile aid. I will deal with this item when it is time to introduce your puppy to 'shot'.

1   This chapter is perhaps the most important in the book. You must . . . understand that you are not training the puppy, so much as laying the foundation for future training. You have been developing and humanising him – there is a big difference. If you make a big thing of these exercises you are trying to train the puppy, and he is too young. However, if you have followed the instructions, ie played with him and incorporated a few exercises into his daily routine, you will have developed his will to please and encouraged him to have confidence. In the first instance you are liable to make the puppy unsure, nervous and inhibited, but in the second instance your puppy will be confident, outgoing and eager to please.

2   The name of the game is relax; if you are uptight and anxious your anxiety will transfer to the puppy.

3   Do not make a ritual of anything. A short pleasant interlude is of much more value than an hour's exercise, for a very obvious reason. The longer the puppy is out with you, the more likely he is to be bored and get distracted, and thus disobey you.

4   Do not demonstrate your puppy's prowess to your friends.

5   Do not listen to your friends' advice.

6   Do not throw endless objects for the dog to retrieve.

7   Do not chase him if he runs away. Attract his attention and run off in the opposite direction, he will then chase after you, giving you the opportunity to praise him rather than chastise him.

8   Educate the wife and children.

9   Keep him happy. If at any time he shows signs of nerves or fear, you are overdoing it. Get him out and play with him until he is full of bounce again.

10 Take him about with you.

11 Do not under any circumstances let curiosity get the better of you and fire a shot over him to see if he is gun-shy, the tympanic membrane of the ear has not fully developed yet. Very few dogs are gun-shy; it is usually hereditary and

enlightened breeding policies over the past few years have gone a long way to eradicate it. But very many dogs are gun-nervous due to having a shot fired over them too close and at too tender an age. All in good time. So don't take the puppy to the local clay-busting club. And don't trail him around game fairs or field trials, tests and the like. Remember he is just a baby.

CHAPTER THREE

Real Training Begins

HAND TRAINING

Your puppy is now around 6 or 7 months old and, if you have observed his behaviour during his earlier puppyhood, you should by now have a fairly good idea as to his temperament. Furthermore if you have been consistent in the development period he should be a biddable puppy, but nevertheless happy and confident in your company.

The ground you choose for hand training should be devoid of game. There should be no distractions such as people, other dogs or livestock; therefore, the local park is most definitely out. Release the puppy from the lead and give him a short scamper for a few minutes.

It is quite permissible to throw a dummy for him, perhaps once every other training session – once only, do not overdo it. This retrieve should be given before the training session begins, it will keep him keen and alert. Never, never, give a dog a retrieve after a training session for the puppy will be tired, and the chances of him being bored and disinterested even to the point of refusing to pick up the dummy are increased.

As in all training, what has gone before is incorporated in the lessons that follow, thus the puppy's knowledge should grow like a snowball rolling downhill. Lessons should be kept as simple as possible in the early stages, to increase your chances of success. They should be short in duration but given as often as possible. Ten minutes per day is of far greater value than four hours on a Saturday afternoon. Remember the longer a training session is, the greater the chances of the puppy getting bored and consequently disobeying you. On the other hand if the lesson is short the puppy should be keen and alert to your demands, and your chances of success are greater.

It is perfectly possible to train a dog from A to Z without ever having to degenerate into giving him physical chastisement. If I have to give a spaniel, even a hard dog, physical chastisement, that is a bad day. Even if it solves the immediate problem it represents failure, because in some way I have failed him in the preceding lessons. I have done something wrong. The situation should not have arisen.

As I have said before, I do not subscribe to the view that there is such a thing as a bad dog, rather that he is a victim, like many children, of his environment. It follows that in the majority of cases, when things have gone wrong, some way back along the learning chain there must have been a flaw. I say in the majority of cases, for there are dogs who, by bad breeding, or a mating that has not clicked, have a serious inherent fault, even to the point of making them untrainable. However, in saying so we must never fall into the trap of making that an excuse for our inability to train them. Many dogs have been brought to me as nervous wrecks, having been rejected by other trainers, the owners having been told they were untrainable. Yet in time with gentle handling, and a lot of hard work and frustration on my part, they have turned out very good working animals. In many cases I have sold young puppies because they were temperamentally unsuited to a public kennel existence, but would blossom in the family situation. This is most prevalent in the sensitive animal.

I suspect that to the novice trainer the sensitive type of dog is a blessing in disguise, for after all he has not got the experience to train a bold, hard-going dog. Such dogs, being as all dogs are, very astute, are quick to realise and take advantage of this. And there we have it: the classic case of the dog training the owner. The sensitive animal on the other hand, tends to be what we call an honest dog and is very often an intelligent one at that. Such dogs, if they are brought along gently, ultimately make the most efficient workers.

On many occasions I myself have sent dogs home as being unsuitable for training, who have ultimately made the grade. The professional is in difficulties here, for in four short weeks he has to assess a puppy and decide if it is worth the owner spending a lot of money on it. He tends to play safe for the sake of his

50

reputation, for woe betide the trainer who takes a dog for training and sends back a dud. Very few people ever hear of the good dogs that he has trained, but the world, or so it seems at times, gets to know all about the failures.

The amateur, in the one-dog one-man situation, has a great advantage over the professional. He has one dog to concentrate on. He has the time to lavish his pupil with attention and love; therefore all that he requires is guidance in the training of his pupil. By now your puppy should devour you with his eyes. He should think you are absolutely wonderful, the one and only person in his life. If you follow the instructions in this book, step by step you should be perfectly capable of training the average puppy to a very high degree. Bear in mind also your puppy is not being wrenched away from home at the tender age of 6 months into a strange kennel. His development undergoes no traumatic change, but is a gradual transition into a training situation in familiar surroundings.

We will begin by teaching the puppy to sit and stay at distance. I want you to 'hup' the puppy by the method described in Chapter 2. Always use the same command. Once he is 'hupped', take one to three steps backwards with your hand raised, palm outwards, to the puppy, repeating, 'Hup'. 'Hup'. This should be done very slowly with your eyes fixed on a spot just above and between his eyes. Avoid staring into a dog's eyes, he doesn't like it. When you have managed to retreat a few feet, walk the two or three steps forward and immediately make a great fuss of him. His natural reaction when you commence this exercise will be to get up from his 'hupped' position and come towards you. Immediately he looks as though this is his intention, step towards him and repeat in a firm voice, 'Hup'. If he belly-crawls or gets up and gets to you, have patience, try not to frighten him, take him by the scruff and put him back in the same spot. Repeat the exercise, but do not make a long job of it for it is a dicey one. If at first you do not succeed, time enough to try another day. Let him have a short scamper, call him up to you with a whistle, and make a fuss of him. You will find that if you are firm but gentle he will soon get the message. As soon as you succeed let him have another short scamper, call him up on the whistle and praise him.

HUP

GO TO THE RIGHT

GO TO THE LEFT

GET OUT

Making signals clear

A dog kept outside, away from the distractions of the family scene, is a far easier dog to train

When the puppy returns to you with the object, you must show him that you are pleased with him

Dogs are born escapologists

Try to understand how the dog is reacting. Does he understand, is he playing the fool, why did he give a jump and run off a few yards when he was near that hedge, is there something there that gave him a fright? Remember, a paperbag moving in the wind is perfectly understandable to you but to him it is alive, it represents danger and the fear of the unknown; therefore try not to be impatient, but to understand and act accordingly. Try to think like your dog at all times.

Whether you have success or not during the first few days, do not overdo it. Make these sessions short. Sooner or later you will succeed and then you can proceed further. Don't rush it, the puppy must learn this lesson to perfection for this is the cornerstone of training. Until you can sit a puppy down and leave him at distance until he is called up to you, there is little point in trying to progress further. Once you have succeeded, you may proceed by increasing the backward steps by one or two, never more, each day, until you can leave him on the drop about 12–14ft away.

Each session should take the same form, ie a short scamper, a small retrieve, 'Hup', walk backwards, return to him and praise him. Always wind up on a successful note, always give him a pat and tell him he is a· good dog before you leave him in his kennel. Never leave a dog brooding or unhappy. You must always try to dwell on success and play down failure. The prime object is to keep him happy, but also to get compliance with your wishes.

Once you have achieved this standard you may proceed to calling him up from the drop position to the short, sharp, rapid 'peep, peep' signal on your whistle. However, you must be careful how you go about it. Always keep him on the drop for a few seconds before calling him up to you. Every other time you walk away and face him, instead of calling him up with the whistle, you should walk slowly back to him and praise him. This will prevent him anticipating, that is getting up from the drop and coming to you as he sees your hand moving up to your mouth with the whistle. Do not be lazy and skimp this or you will find that you will be back to square one in no time at all.

Once again you must incorporate this lesson with the puppy's daily routine, though as with all future lessons the format is the same. In this way you are increasingly able to vary the contents of the lesson and thus keep it interesting as time goes on. It helps if you can get a different venue every now and then, as a dog soon gets stale if he is on the same patch of ground each day. By now he should be running around, eager to investigate everything and anything that takes his interest. He should have his nose down, especially on ground where you have recently cleared ground game off, as previously described.

QUARTERING

This is an aspect of training which some trainers appear to have great difficulty with. Indeed on more than one occasion I have been told that the only way they found successful was to throw pieces of biscuits first to one side and then the other as they walked the ground. I have never subscribed to this as I believe it could result in teaching the dog to potter. There is nothing worse than a time-wasting, pottering hunting dog.

First, if possible, find a piece of ground which is fairly open with some light ground cover, ie sparse rushes, rough grass, heather or bracken. Keep away from thick cover such as gorse bushes at this stage for you want your spaniel in sight at all times. Furthermore the object of this exercise is to put a pattern of ground treatment into the dog. You will never manage this in gorse bushes or any heavy ground cover such as brambles.

Walk the ground game off in the manner previously described: then, after returning to the car and getting your puppy, release him and tell him to 'get on'. Always proceed into the wind, so that the scent will waft towards him. Now he should go bounding out to one side or the other. Using the whistles that you use for the recall, give one short sharp 'peep', call his name and indicate with your arm the opposite way to that which he has been taking, at the same time walking in that direction yourself. If all goes well he should come trotting or running across you. As soon as he has progressed past you, give another short sharp 'peep' on the same whistle, and if need be call his name if he does not respond. Once again indicate the opposite direction to that in which he is going, and walk in that direction yourself. He should once again come bounding past you. As you proceed

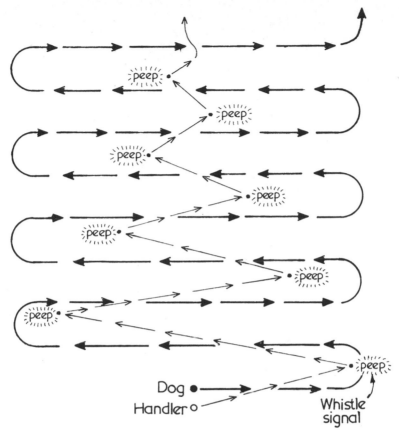

peep

peep

peep

peep

peep

peep

peep

peep

Dog ●——➤
Handler ○

Whistle
signal

Quartering exercises: it may take many weeks of constant practice
before the handler reaches the stage when he can proceed forward in a
straight line

forward in this zig-zag fashion you should find it relatively
simple to control the dog in a fairly methodical pattern. If you
do this each lesson for about 10 minutes you will find as time
goes on that you can narrow your own zig-zag pattern into a
fairly straight line until you are walking slowly forward. But,
and this is important, never throughout a spaniel's life degenerate
to walking forward at too fast a pace. In other words give the
dog time to work his ground at all times, or you will soon destroy
any pattern you have put into him.

Do not blow the whistle for the sake of blowing it. As time
goes on you will find that if you have been consistent and

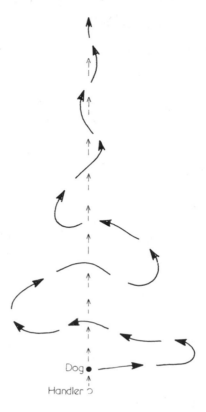

Dog ●

Handler ɔ

This is what will happen if you move forward too quickly: the dog
does not get time to work his ground

turned the dog at roughly the same distance from you each time,
he will begin to turn by himself, only requiring reminding every
now and then. But do keep your eye at all times on the dog, for
if you are inattentive he will quickly realise it and take advantage
of it.

Now and then you will find that he will pull out in front of
you, probably with his nose down on a foot scent, this is known
as 'lining'. Recall him on the whistle with your two short sharp
'peep, peeps', and as he comes back to you swing him off in the
direction you want him to go. You are now well on the way to
a dog that will work a methodical pattern with the aid of
whistles, within shot at all times. Whilst engaged in this lesson

58

it is a good idea, but only now and then, to catch his eye, raise your hand, and call 'Hup'. Chances are he will drop, and if and when he does, walk slowly up to him and praise him. Don't do this too often however, or you may find the dog will start to anticipate it to the detriment of his concentration on hunting, and become sticky and unsure.

Some authorities advocate the use of check cords for teaching quartering. This contrivance simply consists of a long piece of cord approximately 30ft long which is attached around the dog's neck, so that while the dog is running about a sharp short tug on the cord will turn him, whilst simultaneously you give a short 'peep' on the whistle. These same authorities also recommend it for steadying a dog to rabbits. At the risk of appearing arrogant I must say this, that these authorities either have not given much thought to a dog's thinking processes, or they do not credit him with very much sense. The dog is well aware of the restriction on his liberty, he knows that he has to comply with your wishes whilst he is tethered at the end of 30ft of cord, he also knows that he does not have to comply with your wishes once the cord is removed. Not only are these authorities encouraging the dog to do wrong once he is released from the cord, they are illustrating all too clearly to all and sundry their own anxieties in relation to the training of dogs. Having tried this gimmick many years ago I swiftly came to the conclusion that it was an abomination designed by some back-room boy with a diabolical sense of humour in an effort to drive trainers mad with frustration, for it snags on every tuft of grass or twig and wraps itself around your legs. The whole affair quickly deteriorates into chaos, as the dog goes first one way then the other and the cord becomes tangled up in half the surrounding countryside including the handler. As to steadying a dog to rabbits with it, I tend to credit the dogs I breed with the sense to know when their movements are restricted.

In my opinion any trainer who has to resort to the use of a check cord should go back to square one and learn how to hand train properly. For if the dog is allowed to see the rabbit when and only when he is 100 per cent steady to the drop whistle the trainer, provided his reactions are quick enough, should be able to drop the dog to the first rabbit encountered, in which

59

case the check cord is an unnecessary contrivance.

These check cords may be bought, and are becoming more sophisticated as time goes on. Indeed the latest one the manufacturers have put on the market has been designed to keep a steady tension on the dog's neck, thus avoiding snagging on grass etc. Whilst this is an improvement it still does not eradicate the basic problem, ie the dog knows he is attached to it because he feels the pressure, and he knows when he is not attached to it; therefore it defeats its own ends.

A few problems may arise whilst teaching a dog to quarter his ground. A sensitive puppy (whether it is hereditary sensitivity, induced by the trainer's impatience to get on, by his rough impatient handling, or a combination of all three) is inclined, when any new exercises are introduced, to feel insecure and to display his insecurity in many ways. Thus, commonly, in quartering training, after you have turned him a few times on the whistle or even sooner, he will slow his pace and look at you warily with his tail between his legs; he may even stop and just stand there looking at you. In some cases he may manifest his lack of confidence by coming back and sitting down in front of you. The answer to all insecurity is reassurance. Encourage him, stroke him and speak to him in a soft, soothing happy tone. Normally he will work himself through this stage, for it is purely and simply a lack of confidence. Nevertheless you are walking on eggs, so if after a few days sessions he is not progressing, relax the quartering exercises.

Ask yourself where you have gone wrong, is there scent on the ground? Are the scenting conditions right? The question of scent is a very complicated one; however suffice it to say at this point that any extremes of weather are bad for scent, and therefore will not encourage a young inexperienced dog to bustle about. Should you persist in quartering exercises in adverse weather conditions you will only make matters worse. It is almost impossible to get a young dog hunting if there is no scent. Ask yourself whether you are making too much noise about it, try not to be continually distracting the puppy by talking to him. I very rarely speak to a dog whilst I am giving him quartering lessons.

Do not take the dog out during the day if there is a heat

wave. If you must hunt him, do so first thing in the morning whilst the dew is still on the grass, otherwise don't be afraid to let him have a holiday. A short rest, far from doing harm, will in the majority of cases do a power of good.

Scent is dealt with in Chapter 11, meanwhile try to look at the situation as it must seem to the dog. If normally he goes at a fair pace and one day appears to be much slower, you must ask yourself is he going slow through lack of confidence or is there no scent? On scentless days it is better to keep the sessions short. This is why I like to use 'gamey' ground for quartering lessons, with the game cleared off beforehand.

If you always in the early stages of training hunt your dog into the wind (up-wind beat), your dog should naturally, in turning, turn with nose into the wind. If not he may develop into a down-wind turner, which a good trial judge of any experience will spot immediately and mark you down for. There-fore down-wind turning is extremely undesirable if you intend running your dog in trials, although it may not be considered such a fault if you are training him for a shooting companion. Nevertheless it is worth remembering that if you persist in hunting a dog in a down-wind beat, ie with the wind behind you, this will encourage him in this respect. Therefore, for the time being, try as much as possible to work him into the wind. I will deal in due course with wind tactics, until then you must try to hunt him into the wind at all times.

Some trainers like to use a ploughed field for quartering sessions. Crossing the field with the furrows running from left to right, the dog tends to utilise the bottom of the furrow to run on. Certainly this may tend to tidy up a dog's pattern, but once again do not overdo this as it would tend to make the dog treat his ground in a windscreen-wiper pattern, which although not all that important from the shooting-dog angle, might at a field trial cast a doubt in the judge's mind as to the efficiency of his nose, and therefore his game-finding capabilities.

INTRODUCTION TO WATER

I cannot emphasise strongly enough the need for tact in introduc-ing a puppy to water. Do not throw him in. Choose a warm day in summer and a slow-moving stream, pond or river with gradually sloping banks. I have read that some trainers sit on the bank and throw biscuits into the shallows in the hope that the puppy will run in to pick up the food. Having tried this without any success whatsoever I came to the conclusion that my puppies are either too intelligent to risk their life in this strange new element for such a meagre reward, or they are too well fed. However, the solution is quite simple and it is hard to imagine why these same trainers have not thought of it too. I just don my fishing waders and wander unconcernedly about the shallows whilst the puppy romps around the edge. In this way curiosity usually quickly overcomes his uncertainty as to this unusual element, and he soon gets his feet wet. If I can get his feet to leave the bottom and him paddling, even for a moment, on the first outing, I call it a day and make a great fuss of him. On the second or third outing I gradually wade deeper until he is out of his depth and then coax him up to me; as soon as he reaches me I wade on to the bank and praise him. In nine cases out of ten this works.

Occasionally a puppy just does not have the confidence to swim. Surprisingly this is much more prevalent in retriever breeds than in spaniels. In such a case, once he is running up and down in the shallows – and he must enter of his own free will – it does no harm to take him gently by the scruff with the left hand (I am right-handed) and, supporting him under the chin with the right hand, gradually steer him out of his depth for only a few strokes of his feet. Mind you, you mustn't overdo it; great care must be taken not to frighten the puppy. But in this way he soon gains confidence and grows to look forward to his excursions to the river or pond.

If one has to use one's car on these outings it is a bit off-putting, but many years ago my wife came up with what I thought, and still think, was a brilliant idea – we put the dog into an old mailbag after he had a swim. At first he was not too keen, however in a very short time he grew to realise its benefits and would jump into it on command. This bag has eyelets around the top and by simply threading a cord through the eyelets and around an old dog collar, the dog was held securely in the voluminous sack with his head poking out. His body heat did the rest and he was warm and dry as toast in a very short time indeed. Imagine my chagrin a few years later on seeing similar bags on the market and selling like hot cakes.

SUMMARY

1 Do not nag the dog.
2 Take your time, dogs tend to learn by fits and starts. Let him come on in his own time, he must enjoy being out with you.
3 If things are not going too well do not persevere that day, give him something easy to do, something you are sure he will do, then call it a day.
4 If so and so's dog down the road is further on than yours, forget it. Who knows, trouble may be just around the corner for him. Don't push your luck for this is not a race.
5 If during quartering lessons you notice that every once in a while your dog makes a cast from right to left or left to right behind you, do not draw his attention to it for this is a manifestation of lack of confidence. Left alone he will usually work his way out of it by himself.
6 If for some unknown reason your dog suddenly refuses to hunt – this is very common in a sensitive dog – do not push him. Relax all training for a few weeks, each day taking him for a walk where there is a scent. Watch for signs of his beginning to go again. The trouble may be too much whistle, so that the dog is wondering what you want from him and is naturally uncertain. Ask yourself if you are overdoing things. Remember he is just a puppy, give him a bit of leeway, relax and let him play.

CHAPTER FOUR

Around 8 or 9 Months Old

If all has gone well with the training lessons described in Chapter 3, your puppy should be happy and confident when out with you. As stated before, do not pressure him; take your time, play with him, be relaxed, and he will be relaxed. If you have achieved relaxation of mind in yourself, you should now have him sitting at distance, coming bounding up to you when and only when you call him with the whistle; sitting to the command 'Hup', and/or the raised hand; turning to a single 'peep' on the whistle and if you have done the job well without too much distraction or speed, be working his ground fairly methodically.

Speed is of no real importance at this stage; it is far more important that he is not too slow or hesitant. This is a manifestation of anxiety, and probably you are cramming him. If it becomes apparent that he is hesitant, slow, or showing symptoms of anxiety in other ways, then relax all training, take him out each day, play with him and give him plenty of praise, the object being to build up his confidence again. Once this new confidence is achieved he will once more begin to scamper around with some zest. You can now recommence training, but take it easy, for he has shown you that he is sensitive and requires gentle handling. On the other hand if he is slow but his tail is wagging and his nose is on the ground, obviously he is not anxious. Don't worry about this, if necessary we can speed him up when the time comes. At least if he is slow at this stage, yet happy, he is manageable.

STEADINESS TO THE THROWN DUMMY

It is essential at this juncture to get him 100 per cent steady to the thrown dummy, ie the fall. It is really quite simple, and there are various methods. You may, when you first take him out of his kennel, proceed as usual to a spot where there are no distractions. Keeping him on the lead, make him 'hup', holding the lead with a bit of slack on it, and throw the dummy straight out in front of him. He will, as he has been doing, rush out to get it. Be ready, and as you throw it say 'Hup' in a clear voice again, as he is pulled up with a jerk at the end of the lead. Pull him back into the sitting position beside you, and repeat, 'Hup'. Crouch down beside him, stroke him and repeat over and over 'Hup, good boy, hup', for about 5 to 10 seconds, quietly removing the lead, at the same time grasping him firmly by the scruff. When you have him sitting quietly, send him for the dummy with the command, 'Dead'. When he delivers it to hand make a great fuss of him, replace the lead and repeat the same exercise again. No more during this session. Carry on as usual, ie give him a short scamper, call him up to you with the whistle, sit him down, walk away, hesitate, walk back to him, praise him, give him a short 'Hunt', then put the lead on and take him home.

You will find that most puppies grasp this lesson quite quickly. The next step is to drop the puppy as usual, walk away from him a few yards, face him and, keeping him on the drop, throw the dummy in full view of him but away from and behind you. If you make a practice of keeping your eye on the puppy, throwing the dummy up and over your head behind you, keeping your hand in the air and calling 'Hup' simultaneously, this will assist you in keeping him steady to the fall. Be prepared to get between him and the dummy if he breaks from the drop and goes after it before you have given him the command.

It is important that you intercept him on his way past you. If you manage this, take him by the scruff quietly back to the drop spot and, pressing his bottom on the ground, repeat 'Hup' again and again. Leaving him on the drop, back away until you reach the dummy and, keeping your eye on him, and repeating 'Hup', if he looks as if he is going to break, pick it up walk back to him; give him a pat for remaining on the drop. Once again leaving him on the drop, proceed as before. If you succeed this time, make a great fuss of him, then hunt him on.

If the dog breaks and gets to the dummy, don't rant and rave at him or make any fuss at all. Let him retrieve the dummy to you, accept it, but make nothing of it, give him a short hunt, drop him and start all over again. Patience; he will get there in the end. If you have given him enough practice on the lead you should not have much trouble, as it is only another progression. However, be careful, this can be a dicey aspect of training. Occasionally through mishandling a puppy will get a 'mental block' regarding this exercise, and some will remain on the drop refusing to go out for the dummy on the command 'Dead'. Others can be put off retrieving altogether. Remember, little and often. You now have enough scope to ring the changes so keep each lesson varied, try to retain his interest and thus keep him happy, in this way you should keep him keen.

INTRODUCTION TO SHOT

Your puppy should be around 8 or 9 months old by now. Don't worry if he is older, you are not taking too long, this is not a race. I have found that the slow learner is usually the best at the end of the day. The puppy that tends to pick up a new lesson quickly can just as quickly forget it, one day throwing caution to the winds and consequently his training in one fell swoop is back to square one. I mention age purely to emphasise that he should not be younger on commencing with this exercise.

The first time you introduce him to shot, it is a good plan to have some responsible person with you that the dog knows. Take him to his usual training ground if it is not in close proximity to a conifer wood, high walls, buildings, steep-sided valleys or anything liable to produce an echo. Sit him down on the lead, which is held by the person assisting you. Leave him there with the assistant and walk away approximately 30yd. Facing him, raise your hand in the fashion you use when dropping him at distance, fire one shot and note his reaction. Walk back to him and make a great fuss of him. Ask your assistant what he or she noted when you fired the shot, and this assistant should also reassure the dog when the shot is fired. If all has gone well there should be little or no reaction from the dog to the report from the starter pistol at this distance.

Whilst some dogs do not like the sharp crack that a starter

pistol makes, I would consider it most unusual if at this distance in open country there was any more than the slightest indication that he had even heard the shot. Should there be little or no reaction, then obviously the dog is not all that concerned, consequently it is safe to reduce the distance each day by a few feet until he is quite blasé about the noise. Do not at any time during the training be tempted to fire more than one shot per session. If possible, for the first few exercises have your assistant with you, but if for one reason or another this is not possible, provided the dog is obviously not bothered about shot and you are careful to observe his reactions each time, and you do not decrease the distance too drastically, you should be able to manage on your own by simply leaving him on the drop as in previous lessons. This exercise is one of the few for which I advocate the giving of an edible reward, but only if you think it necessary.

If on the other hand things do not go well, this will manifest itself on the first one or two shots. If the dog is obviously very disturbed about the report I advise you to stop the shot lessons immediately. It may be gun-nervousness in which case, provided you do not push things at this stage, you should be able to solve it. If on the other hand the puppy is gun-shy, you have been most unfortunate, for there is no cure for this. This is an inherent fault, whereas gun-nervousness is usually induced.

No doubt by the time you have reached this stage you have grown attached to your puppy. However it has to be said, if he is gun-shy he is useless for the purpose you purchased him for. Consequently you have to decide whether you purchase another puppy or not, and if you do, what of the one you have already got? This is a dilemma which I cannot solve for you. I can only sympathise.

But under no circumstances should a gun-shy dog or bitch be bred from. If, however, the problem is gun-nervousness, then all that is required is tact and patience, plus a little effort. A well known cure is to fire one shot from a fair distance away each day, immediately before feeding him. Thus he will associate the shots as a signal of good things to come, and you can gradually decrease the distance each day until you can fire a shot from quite nearby and, instead of uncertainty, the dog displays symptoms of excitement and anticipation. On noting this reaction you may then proceed with the exercises relating to shot, bearing in mind once again however, that having been forewarned you should be forearmed. Play safe.

You should now have your puppy 100 per cent steady to the thrown dummy, ie you can throw it in any direction and he will remain on the drop, and he is showing no concern with regards to shot. The next progression in training is to leave the dog on the drop, and walk out about 30yd. Facing him, raise your hand holding the pistol, fire a shot, and at the same time throw the dummy out and away from him. As before, he must on no account be allowed to break from the drop. On achieving this, walk slowly back to him, praise him, wait a second or two, then send him with the command 'Dead. Get out'.

Remember always to incorporate the retrieve at the beginning of each training session, never at the end of it. All new exercises such as introduction to shot etc are incorporated in the daily training schedule, never on their own. End each lesson on a successful note thus keeping the puppy happy. Once again, do not be in too much of a hurry to get on to something new. Always make sure that each lesson is well and truly absorbed by the puppy before progressing on to the next. However, be careful not to treat it like a drill sergeant; this is not a barrack square. Be relaxed. Remember that as long as the dog obeys and as long as when you give a command you insist that it is complied with, you can afford a little relaxation with the puppy.

The people who have trouble training a dog are the people who are forever nagging it, giving constant commands in situations where it should be obvious that the dog is not going to, or at the very least is going to be reluctant to, comply with them. Rather than be constantly on at the dog, it is far better to let him scamper about, let him investigate, let him play, but keep him in sight where, if necessary, you can call him back before a situation develops. In this way the puppy will look forward eagerly to his daily excursions with you, he will be attentive and eager to please, not a pup who is so used to hearing you prattle on that he takes no notice, with the result that if you allow him to get away with it, he will get worse and worse. If you allow him a bit of leeway and open your mouth only when it is required, the dog will take notice, and if you show him that when you make a sound it is to be obeyed – in other words you are consistent – he will develop into a receptive dog and will be the easier trained.

CARE OF THE COAT

Whilst out hunting, your dog will collect all manner of things in his coat. It is essential that you show him you care for him by, after every outing, taking a quick look at his paws for thorns, checking his coat, paying particular attention to his ears for bits of bramble, nettle, twigs, thorns, burrs etc, and remove any matted hair.

High summer can be a problematical time for the dog and his owner. Long-haired dogs such as the spaniel provide an ideal habitat for fleas and lice, especially the kennel dog, although house dogs can bring them in as well. However if a weekly check is made, and if at the first signs of unwelcome visitors preventative treatment is undertaken, the problem can be overcome very easily. I have found that a bath is far more efficient than flea and louse powders. Gamexaine or Alugan readily available from your vet, added to the water, will not only get rid of these present pests but will kill any that may hatch out over the next few weeks. Needless to say in cases of heavy infestation, repeated baths are indicated.

Another pest at this time of year is the sheep tick. These are little brown creatures that embed themselves in the dog's flesh, gorging themselves with his blood, until they resemble a small football about the size of a pea. The natural reaction is to try to brush them off. All that will be achieved by this is that the body will separate from the head which will remain embedded in the skin, and may then cause a suppurating sore. By far the best method of dealing with them is to paint them with nail varnish remover, leaving it on overnight. They will then die and drop off, leaving only the minutest of punctures which will heal within hours.

I have never experienced any difficulty in training a dog to jump if training is the right word, for I do not have any specifically built 'jumps' as such, relying more on the drystone walls in my area. The method is simple when the dog is physically capable – I just climb a wall in the ordinary course of a day and leave him to scramble over as best he can. He learns eventually.

However, with regard to obstacles of any kind, you should insist that the dog remains 'hupped' before negotiating it, and immediately after surmounting it. Not only does this give you a measure of control whilst negotiating the obstacles yourself, but prevents a dog going flying over objects into possible danger. Furthermore it prevents him from jumping obstacles where you would not want him to go. Never at any time do I allow a dog to jump barbed wire, as this can inflict the most atrocious injuries.

SUMMARY

1 Speed at this stage of training is of no real importance; there is no real cause for alarm if he appears to lack drive, for at the moment, he has only instinct to motivate him, he does not know what he is hunting for. Once he has seen game, he will speed up considerably.
2 If he should sight game before he is ready for it, you may well find that he will be much more difficult to control.
3 If the puppy should give a violent start on hearing the starter pistol the first few times, increase the distance the next day. Do not be tempted into thinking that multiple shots will cure the problem by familiarising the puppy to the sound. Play safe.
4 There is a very true saying regarding the training of gun dogs, ie three years to make, three minutes to mar. By one hasty unthinking act you can undo all your good training in a few seconds. Let consistency be your keynote.

Hup!

Make your hand signals clear

Get on

Once a dog is physically capable he will learn to jump quite easily

CHAPTER FIVE

More Is Expected

By the time you have reached this stage of his training, your dog will have changed considerably. He is still a pup, but he has grown, not only physically but mentally as well, and whilst you should never lose sight of the fact that he is still a puppy, much more can be expected from him.

DROPPING TO THE WHISTLE

This is a refinement, albeit one essential in a well-trained dog, which appears to mystify the average shooting man, and yet in conjunction with what has gone before in this book it is really very simple.

As usual, in the process of giving your dog a training session incorporating all that has gone before, you come to leaving your dog on the drop. In addition to the raised right hand and command 'Hup', you give him a short, sharp, single blast on the thunderer whistle and at all times in the future, when dropping the dog, you add this single whistle signal. You will find that he will grasp the idea very rapidly, and as time goes on you will be able to drop him at distance with the whistle and raised hand, dispensing with the word 'Hup', which will only be used at close quarters in a low voice from then on.

Because different dogs react to new commands in a wide variety of ways, difficulty may be experienced in introducing this new 'sound' into the dog's training curriculum. This is quite rare, nevertheless it does occur. At the first utterance of the stop whistle whilst the dog is hunting, he will in all probability hesitate. Usually on seeing the raised hand and hearing the command 'Hup' he will drop. Occasionally, however, especially with the sensitive dog, instead of dropping he will come running back to you. The dog is uncertain, but do not start wild gesticulation and repeated blasts on the stop whistle, for this will only frighten him further. He needs reassurance, so soothe him and pat him. Remember he has never heard this whistle 'sound' before, and you cannot expect an immediate response to it. If he drops, he has dropped to either the word 'Hup' or/and the raised hand signal. Eventually he will connect the stop whistle with the command, but not straight away.

If after introducing him to the stop whistle, he shows signs of anxiety or uncertainty then, as in all training, you must be flexible. It is a simple matter in this instance to introduce him to the stop whistle at feeding times, together with the raised hand and the verbal command 'Hup'. In nine cases out of ten this will solve the problem. You may then incorporate the stop-whistle command into the actual training.

DROPPING TO SHOT

Once your dog is proficient at dropping to whistle and hand-signals and is blasé about the pistol, it is a simple matter to practise dropping to shot in conjunction with the whistle command.

Hunt the dog as usual and, when you think it is convenient to drop him whilst he is hunting, raise your hand, give the whistle signal and immediately fire a shot. He will, if you have not rushed things, drop like a stone. As time goes on you will find that he will drop to the shot alone, nevertheless it is as well to play safe and give the whistle signal at all times as well. A good maxim with this lesson and the stop-whistle lesson is moderation in all things. Do not continually stop the dog whilst he is hunting, otherwise you will confuse him, even to the point of stopping him hunting altogether. If you drop him once with the whistle command, and once more by the whistle in con-junction with the pistol shot, that is twice in any one training session; that, to my mind, should be quite sufficient to bed it in over a period of a few weeks.

A word here about whistle signals. You will note that I have emphasised with each signal that it should be short and sharp; this does not necessarily mean loud, but it does mean short and sharp. The reason is perfectly simple. A short, sharp command carries urgency; it means *now*. Sloppy commands mean sloppy responses, and in a field trial can mean the difference between winning and defeat. Certainly, whether it be in the shooting situation or the field trial, it can mean the difference between a dog remaining steady or, if he is in the habit of having long-drawn-out commands, deciding to give chase. So 'spit it out' at all times. Through the years I have unconsciously developed the habit of pressing the tip of the tongue against the whistle, and as I blow releasing the tongue rather like trying to get rid of a speck of tobacco from the tip.

Very often I am asked, why two whistles, wouldn't one utilised for all three whistle commands be sufficient? The answer is of course, yes. Many handlers use only one whistle to good effect and find it much more convenient, since it eliminates the inevitable fumbling which may result in a 'hot corner' if two whistles are employed. Nevertheless I prefer the use of two whistles because, in my opinion, the one whistle utilised for all three commands – turn, recall and drop – tends to encourage misinterpretation in the excitement of the moment in the 'hard going' dog. There is no possible room for mistake if one whistle is used exclusively for the drop, saving the other for the less important signals.

CHASTISEMENT AND CORRECTION

At this juncture a word about chastisement would not go amiss as it applies to the older puppy and will supplement the notes on punishment of the very young puppy in Chapter 2. Not a nice subject, and one that many writers tend to avoid, or at least are vague about. Nevertheless if success is to be achieved in the training of dogs, it is of vital importance that the trainer understands fully when, where and how it should be administered. As I have said earlier, the keynote at all times is consistency. With the majority of sensitive dogs it is perfectly possible to train them in the manner described in this book without, or with the very minimum, of correction – provided of course that the training is bedded in properly as you go along. I would most certainly think very seriously before embarking on physical chastisement of this type of dog. However, not all dogs are sensitive. Nevertheless, whether they are 'hard cookies' or not, the form of chastisement that I use is not likely ever to cow or frighten a dog, but it is very effective.

By bedding in the basics outlined so far in this book, employing the principle little and often and not allowing the dangerous situation to develop, the puppy is protected from temptation until it is second nature for him to obey. Thus I have, on more occasions than not, found that even when the puppy reached the stage where a rabbit was presented to him for the first time, when and only when I considered that he was ready for it, he dropped to the whistle on the 'flush'. Training a gun dog is after all employing the same principles of conditioning reflexes as Pavlov did with his dogs. If more trainers knew this, and employed these principles, chastisement would play little or no part in the training.

Steadiness to ground game appears to be the bugbear of many trainers. In point of fact, I suspect that the simple reason why many English field trialists do not come into Scotland to compete is that Scottish trials tend to be mainly held on rabbits, ie ground game. In England, however, trials tend to be bird trials, and thus do not afford the same degree of temptation for the dogs to chase. It is perfectly feasible for a dog to shine in a bird trial, and indeed even reach the dizzy heights of field trial champion, who may be the wildest, craziest brute when presented to ground game. It is for this very reason that I train all my clients' dogs on ground game first, introducing them to birds on 'picking up' days. A dog trained on ground game can swiftly adapt to working birds, not so a dog trained to flushing birds to the exclusion of experience on fur.

A point to remember: whilst your dog may drop to the first bunny he meets, do not be lulled into a false sense of security, for I have found that the 'danger' bunny is not the first one he encounters, but perhaps the third or fourth. This is the one to really watch out for. The reason is simple, the puppy is subjected to an element of surprise when he meets the first rabbit, for until then he has been hunting instinctively, encouraged by exciting rabbit scent. However, after flushing two or three rabbits, he will begin to connect the scent with the rabbits and will 'hot up' as the scent gets stronger. He will be ready for the 'find', and thus you may experience a little more difficulty in stealing the initiative.

Nevertheless the majority of dogs trained by me, have never chased in their lives. I cannot of course vouch for their behaviour after they have left my care, although many of my clients remark to be on their extraordinary steadiness on ground game. It all adds up to the fact that, should you resist the temptation to push on too fast, you will find that chastisement need not be uppermost in your mind.

Owing to anxiety, far too many amateur trainers adopt the sergeant-major approach to training, continually nagging the dog, both with whistle and voice, until he becomes so used to the cacophony set up he attaches little or no importance to it. He regards it more as an accompaniment, the status quo rather than commands, consequently he becomes whistle and voice deaf, and progressively more independent, so that as a last desperate resort the 'trainer' embarks on a policy of chastisement.

In the majority of cases, probably because the trainer does not wish to overdo it, the rebuke will at first be quite mild, gradually as time goes on becoming more and more severe, all to no avail. What has happened is that the dog has become progressively more immune to the punishment, in other words he has become case hardened, at which point the owner usually just gives up and resigns himself to shooting over a wild dog. There are some, thankfully very few, who degenerate to the point of bestiality in their treatment of the dog. Let me assure you this will achieve nothing, except a life of misery for both the poor animal and the so-called trainer; for if he possess a spark of humanity in him he will suffer from a guilty conscience.

On the other hand, as already mentioned, should the dog be of a sensitive disposition, far from case hardening him this type of treatment will frighten him out of his wits. He will become a 'sticky' lifeless potterer, all through no fault of his own. It is the fault of the trainer.

In the 'dog world', especially in the field trial world, there are many who project the image of being knowledgeable. After watching them for many years and listening to them scattering their pearls of wisdom as to what such and such a dog would get when they got him home, or what so and so's dog needed, and seeing these 'trainers' practising their techniques at sundry times, I came to the conclusion early in my amateur days, that if that was the only way to train a dog I would give up for a more amenable pastime.

For many years I worked with disturbed children, children who had been subjected to every conceivable trauma of life – broken homes, drunkenness, immorality – as well as having been subjected to the most bestial of cruelty imaginable. They were the flotsam and jetsam of human life. Physical chastisement held no fear for them. A room full of these children, from all walks of life, could instill fear in the toughest of men. Indeed many staff in the hospital refused to work with them.

Through the years I found that physical chastisement was of no avail. These children had been subjected to it all to frequently before. They were the product of cruelty and neglect, both mental and physical; they had been case hardened. Nevertheless to effect any cure, control was necessary. The one thing that had been missing in all their lives was a stable background; whereas they knew how to handle violence, consistency tempered with understanding was a new experience. Thus far from experiencing difficulty in establishing a harmonious atmosphere with these children, using consistency as the basis of my dealings with them, I found my task easy, rewarding and very enjoyable.

As with children, the dog is acutely aware of what is just. Therefore the essence of success is (1) understanding; (2) avoiding the dangerous situations; (3) consistency; (4) justice at all times. If you master this then you are well on the way to being a trainer.

I remember a schoolmaster of mine back in the 'good old days' some thirty years ago who, although he had every access to the 'belt', never used it, and yet we never messed him about. Indeed there were masters who bordered on the sadistic, yet had less control than he. His secret was he was consistent. Where the others sometimes only threatened and children being optimists tried it on, if he said something he meant it and, more important, we knew he meant it. He issued a command once. If it was disobeyed, he pulled our ears and it hurt. I consider that to give your spaniel a short tug on the ear is not cruel, not nearly as cruel as laying on a lead which is a common sight in the High Street every day of our lives.

So that is what I suggest. If it is obvious that the dog knows the command you have given him, yet has not complied, he is trying you on. Woe betide you if you let him get away with it. If you give the turn whistle and he does not turn, or turns a few yards further on, this is the thin edge of the wedge. Drop him, walk slowly up to him, do not speak to him, take him by the ear keeping him on the drop, give the ear a sharp tug and give him the turn-whistle signal in the ear. If he should have dropped to the stop whistle and he didn't, or dropped a few yards further on, that it not good enough. Get after him, but do not make a big noise; remember the object is to show him he has done wrong not to frighten him. Take him by the scruff back to where he should have dropped. Drop him on that spot, blow the stop whistle in his ear repeatedly in between saying 'There. Hup-there'. If he has any brains at all, the next time you blow the stop whistle you will get a much smarter response.

With the return whistle the treatment is slightly different. If you have given him the recall signal and he is obviously not paying any attention, you must enforce your will upon him. Failure in this will result in the dog developing into habitually hunting out of shot. You go after him, and take him by the scruff once again. But this time you take a pace backwards, utter the whistle command, and at the same time give him a sharp pull towards you; another pace backwards, whistle command again, pull him in to you again. Repeat this three or four times. Drop him and give the recall signal in his ear a couple of times more to push the message home. You will find that in the majority of cases, without resorting to drastic measures, all but the hardest or dimmest of dogs will get the message, and if you are firm enough all but the insane will come round to your way of thinking eventually.

In this way the majority of dogs can be trained, as opposed to being broken, and no matter what anybody says, including the books, if you have to resort to physical violence to train a dog or any animal, then training ends there and breaking begins. Ask yourself this question, how long would a lion tamer be a lion tamer if he went into the cage and knocked the lion about?

But then there are no lion breakers, just lion tamers.

Unfortunately there are exceptions to every rule. Should you be unfortunate enough to have an exceedingly hard dog – and some dogs on finding hot scent react like one possessed and are completely deaf to all commands – a sharp lesson may be necessary. But if you embark upon physical correction with this type of dog, see that the lesson goes home straight away. In other words, make sure you do not have to do the job twice.

Nevertheless, even with the hardest of dogs it is much better that you train him from A to Z without laying hands upon him. The emphasis, in my methods, is in the avoidance of temptation until the hand training is well and truly absorbed. By this means even the toughest dogs that ever lived can be conditioned in good habits as opposed to bad, even the softest will not have their spirit broken, but you will get obedience and at the same time develop the dog's initiative. If you practise the above doctrines at all times, and are consistent and just, you should, unless he is mentally unstable or neurotic, have a dog capable of doing his work to a very high standard.

Be good to your dog and he will repay you a thousandfold. If you are not feeling right in yourself, or the dog's responses are not as usual, then in all probability he is not feeling right. That's the day to have a day off, don't go rushing blindly on, for you will do more harm than good. Remember, no matter how badly things have gone on a particular day, give him something simple, something that you are sure he will comply with, that you may finish the session on a successful note. This is perhaps one of the most important points to remember in the training of a dog.

SUMMARY

1 If you remember that whenever a new sound is first introduced into the training the dog in all probability will obey the accompanying signal, the signal that you have been using until then. In time the dog will associate the new sound with the old signal and the response required of him. Thus each new 'lesson' is a progression, each is linked to the last, a chain of learning. In this way you will appreciate that if you take short cuts, the chain will break down.

2 There are very few hard dogs around these days so gear your chastisement to the dog's temperament and to the crime. Remember, dogs are acutely aware of what is just and what is not. Make sure that each aspect of training is firmly bedded in before progressing on to the next lesson; this will go a long way in maintaining the bond between you. Know your dog.

3 Be consistent; dogs are supreme optimists and if yours beats you once over any particular command or signal, he will forever try it on with you in that particular aspect of training. It is also extremely important that you are not continually talking to a dog whilst you are training him, for familiarity breeds contempt. Furthermore, for some inexplicable reason dogs respond much more readily to a whistle, so the voice is not going to achieve much anyway. It is far better to keep the verbal commands to a minimum, and in this way if and when you do speak whilst working him, he will be far more likely to take notice. Each time you give a command you present the dog with an opportunity to disobey, so the more results you can get to the minimum of commands the better your training will be.

4 Remember never to chastise the dog in the heat of the moment. If you lose your temper it is far better to count to ten, put the lead on him and take him home.

CHAPTER SIX

The Halfway Stage of Training

ADVANCED DUMMY WORK

If by this stage you have followed the lessons in this book little and often, your puppy will be retrieving the dummy keenly up, and delivering, to hand. We are now going to progress from the canvas dummy to the rabbit-skin dummy. As usual on arrival at the chosen training place you drop the puppy, throw his usual dummy out into light cover such as rough grass, make him wait as usual for a few seconds, then send him for it. On his delivering the dummy, pat him or praise him as usual and immediately throw out the fur dummy; make him wait, then send him for it. In the majority of cases he will pick it immediately. When he does this, get him back to you with the encouragement of the return whistle, the idea being to get the dummy back to you before he stops and starts to play with it. On success, praise him as usual, and no more retrieving this session.

Each subsequent session, if all is going well, carry on with the fur dummy. Remember, all retrieving is done immediately you commence a session, never at the end. We want him keen and fresh. Don't panic if the first few times he gives it a shake or tries to play with it, this is just the novelty of it; but do try to get it back to you as quickly as possible. Only occasionally will a puppy refuse to pick it. Should he so refuse, go out and pick it yourself, call the dog up to you, make a fuss of him, let him sniff the dummy, throw it and immediately send him for it. If once again he refuses it, we must make it more interesting for him and, as in all training, must be versatile. What may be meat for one dog may be poison for another, but in this case I would suggest a half-grown rabbit, shot the day before, ie cold game.

Normally one would not try to short circuit training, but this is an abnormal case and we must pander to it. Nevertheless, if the situation does not warrant it do not try to shorten the fur-dummy training and substitute cold game too soon, for therein lies the danger of inducing hard mouth. In this particular instance we are trying to get the dog on to retrieving fur, it is an exceptional case and demands exceptional measures.

Throw the cold rabbit out in front of the dog and, after a suitable pause, send him for it. As soon as he gets to it, before he has time to sniff it or play with it, give the recall signal, repeat if necessary, and run away from the dog. This is almost bound to succeed. Never use the same rabbit twice and, as soon as success in this exercise is achieved, no more cold game mean-time – revert to the fur dummy.

After four or five sessions the dog should be delivering the fur dummy to hand quite keenly and, remembering that each session should be as varied as possible, you should be giving him practice at perhaps sitting at distance once during a session, giving him a short hunt, dropping him on the whistle, calling him back to you etc.

Now we are going to vary the retrieving. Having put the dog on a lead, you walk him, preferably along a wall at this stage but it is not all that important. Drop the dummy in full view of him, tell him to leave it, walk on, stop, take the lead off and drop him, then back away slowly a few yards with your hand raised, repeating 'Hup' till you are approximately 4yd farther away from him. In other words you have the dummy at approximately 10yd, then the dog, then, at a further 4yd, yourself. He will probably be looking at you, and occasionally slowly looking round in the direction of the dummy, for he will remember it.

At this stage don't keep him on the drop longer than is necessary, just long enough for you to catch his eye and with a forward motion of the raised hand, command 'Dead. Get out, get out'. By the time you have uttered the second command he should have reached the dummy. Each session increase the distance between the dog and the dummy by about 1 or 2yd. The object is to reach the stage when you can send him back approximately 30yd – a gun shot. If you achieve this, experience in the field will set the seal on it and, in conjunction with the lessons which follow, will produce a dog that will handle out to

83

a blind fall with hand-signals and whistles – what some trainers tend to deride as 'sheep dogging', only because, I suspect, that they cannot do it themselves. Believe me, a dog that will handle out to a 'blind' with whistles is a joy to behold, and once you have owned such an animal you will want no other.

You may encounter a little difficulty with this exercise, once again some dogs react entirely differently to others to any new situation. If at any time the dog is having difficulty, shorten the distance between the dog and the dummy. Thus the dog will build up his own confidence, and you can then make it a little more difficult each session – be flexible.

You will find it helpful to commence this lesson walking the dog down the wind. In the early stages, when he only has a few yards to go back into the wind this is not all that important, but it is helpful when he reaches the stage where you are sending him back a considerable distance. He will then have the wind in his face, and consequently the scent will help him in the last few vital yards where success in this is all-important.

At this stage it is important to understand that, whilst as your dog progresses in training each exercise is incorporated into each session, the retrieving exercises are not. This is because some dogs will for ever and a day go rushing out to pick up dummies whereas others get bored with it very easily. Consequently, once again you must play safe. Until now you have been taking the dog out, leaving him on the drop, and throwing a dummy for him. From now on discard this exercise and substitute the go-back retrieve outlined above.

Never forget either that little and often is the order of the day; one go-back exercise in each session, never more. This is quite enough together with the usual quartering practice, plus a drop to whistle or shot or both, then a further short period of hunting, finishing with him remaining on the drop as you walk away, a short pause and you either calling him up to you with the whistle, or returning to him. If all has gone well, it should be praise for the dog, and finish the session for the day. Never overdo anything. If for instance, when you are giving him his usual quartering exercise you are dropping him too often on the whistle, he will begin to anticipate you, and his hunting will begin to get spasmodic. So take it easy, it will pay in the end.

Until now your puppy has only been given the shot from a blank .22 pistol. Now I want you to introduce him to the gun that you would normally use when out shooting, ie 12, 16, 28 or 4.10. Choosing a piece of flat country away from conifers etc, repeat the exercises on shot, namely fire a shot at 30yd from the dog, note his reaction, and decrease the distance daily. This is more of a precautionary measure, for in the majority of cases if a puppy can stand the sharp report of a .22 there is no problem with the duller report of the shotgun. However, just make sure he is not frightened.

It is a good idea if every now and again you carry a gun with you from now on. But leave the cartridges at home, for it is extremely tempting to take a pot-shot at something if you have cartridges with you. All in good time, what we are doing here is getting the dog used to you carrying this object.

Whilst hunting him after he has become proficient at the get-out or go-back retrieving – which incidentally is a good way of speeding up this aspect of a dog's retrieving if it becomes slack in the future – it is quite permissible at this stage to introduce a variation of retrieving. Hunt the dog into the wind, take a dummy out of your bag or pocket without his seeing you, wait your opportunity, throw it out in front of him and, at the same time or a split second after the dummy leaves your hand, drop him with the stop whistle. If, out of the corner of his eye, he catches sight of the dummy falling, there is no harm done, but leaving him on the drop, walk out and pick it up yourself. This will be useful anyway, for it will impress on him that every retrieve is not for him, and that he must at all times wait for the command before he moves. If he has not seen the fall then, as with get-out retrieving, send him for it. Do not start shouting, 'Hi! Lost'. 'Fetch it' etc, you will only confuse the dog. You can help him by taking a step forward occasionally.

As the sessions progress he will get quite good at getting out to the unseen retrieve, but take your time. Your dog is already beginning to achieve a good standard of hand training, but we have still a long way to go. He is most definitely not ready to go shooting for many a long day yet, have patience, practise what has gone before, keep the bounce in him. When throwing the dummy out for the blind retrieve, stop him now and then with the starter pistol. As time goes on he will connect the shot with something to retrieve, and this will become an added inducement.

Vary the retrieves, make them progressively more difficult, but do it gradually. Try to get him out onto varied terrain, ie rough grass, light rushes, bracken or heather. Put the blind retrieves into every conceivable kind of cover. Put one into a ditch or the bottom of a hedge; whilst hunting him in cover put one out into the open. You will find it quite difficult to get a hunting dog to leave the cover and handle out into the open on a blind retrieve. Use the feather dummy and the fur dummy alternately, but keep the lessons interesting.

ADVANCED WATER WORK

By now your dog should be perfectly familiar with water and indeed be a bold swimmer. Retrieving from water should present no problems. Simply sit him down on the bank and give him a marked retrieve, making sure that you pause before you send him. If he is a proficient retriever on land, there should be no difficulty. Never send him more than once on the same day for the same dummy. Later, just as on land, you can ring the changes, ie one retrieve in the water and one on the far bank.

The first few times you place a dummy on the bank, make it easy, not too far to swim and a straightforward marked retrieve. Some time later try one in the water and one on the bank, but make certain of success in the early stages. The command should be the same as on land, ie 'Dead. Get out. Get out'. As his confidence grows with experience in water, you will be able to handle him with whistles together with the appropriate hand-signals exactly as on land, and to any retrieve that circumstance puts your way.

When you and your dog have reached a proficient standard on all that has gone before, you will have reached the half-way stage of training. Although there is still a long way to go, from now on it really gets interesting Nevertheless you must resist the temptation to take him shooting, he is not ready yet. As a sort of test I want you to take him out and sit him down, walk off 50yd or so, turn and walk back to him, give him a short hunt, drop him on the whistle, pause, recall him with the whistle, pause, then hunt him on again. Whilst he is hunting, put out a blind retrieve and simultaneously fire a shot. Did he drop and watch you for instructions? All right, send him for it. Did he deliver it all right? Hunt him on. Drop him to the whistle and a shot, give the command 'Gone away', hunt him on. Recall him. If he comes off with flying colours you are both doing well.

SUMMARY

1 With regard to retrieving, remember that a spaniel is a hunter first and a retriever second. Be flexible and if you are having difficulties with a particular aspect of retrieving, try to think it out. Bear in mind that the better the hunter your dog is, the better his nose. A dog such as this is often very independent. On being sent out for a blind, he may well branch off to the right or left, short of the 'fall'; this is because he is distracted by any pocket of scent. On the other hand, a dog who does not have such efficient scenting powers will be more dependent on you and will wait for your order; consequently he will pick up handling out to a blind much more quickly.

2 It is most important that a young dog does not fail on a 'blind' retrieve; help him even if it means in the early stages of this exercise that you have to walk forward slowly encouraging him all the time, if necessary almost up to the dummy. He must succeed for, should he fail too often, he will begin to disbelieve you when you ask him to get out for an unseen retrieve.

3 Never get angry with him whilst he is looking for a retrieve. Remember, as I have said earlier, a dog's eyesight is different from ours and his horizons are lower and therefore what may be in full view to you may be obscured to him, even by a tussock of grass. A little patience goes a long way.

4 Exaggerate your hand signals so that they are clear to him at distance.

5 Do not take the dog out for training sessions in a 'heat wave'. A short holiday is not going to hurt him. Make sure of such weather conditions to give him water work.

CHAPTER SEVEN

Launchers and Advanced Dummy Work

DUMMY LAUNCHERS

This lesson on dummy launchers is included because I wish to leave nothing out which may be of value to the reader. And, because they have become very popular over the past few years, I feel I should give instruction on their uses and warnings of their abuses. Furthermore, if in the future, as a hobby or to cut your teeth before entering field trials proper, you have a go at field tests, you will find that the dummy launcher is used extensively in these affairs. Therefore, if field tests are your aim it is desirable, if not essential, that your dog at least hears one before entering. There is definitely a difference in the report of a launcher as opposed to anything else. I have well-seasoned performers in the shooting field who do not like the launcher, but have no reservation whatsoever to the gun.

If used with foresight, the launcher can be invaluable, not only in teaching a dog to mark, be steady to shot, fall etc, but because of its versatility in placing retrieves. Also if the dummy is covered with a rabbit skin, by launching it horizontally low along the ground whilst the dog is hunting, it simulates a 'toppled' rabbit very well indeed.

However in introducing this tool to the dog in training, a careful note of the dog's reaction to it must be taken and acted upon. It would be well to treat the first few sessions as if you were introducing the dog to shot all over again, ie fire at 30yd and note reaction; next session, if all is well, fire at a few yards closer, and so on. Proceed warily, the launcher can produce a fearful echo.

Whether you purchase a launcher or not is entirely up to you. I may be in danger of being accused of being old-fashioned in

88

Field-trial winner Lady Mindy, daughter of field-trial winner, Macsiccar
Michele

Carry a gun but leave the cartridges at home in the early stages of training

this, but in my opinion in the hands of the amateur this tool, by virtue of its versatility, is very often abused. I much prefer to rely on the starter pistol and my own ingenuity in placing the fur or feather dummies by hand. If used wisely the dummy launcher can be a tremendous help, but to the one-dog man it is, like a rabbit pen, unnecessary.

I find the launcher cumbersome, either carried in one's hand, or in a bag. In the first instance it is all too easy for the dog to develop the irritating habit of watching you, anticipating, then waiting for the inevitable bang and stop whistle. If not noticed until too late, this habit will ultimately tend to make him sticky in his hunting. In the second instance, whilst hunting a dog I have found it extremely difficult to remove a launcher from my bag without attracting the dog's atention. All things considered, my advice to you is, if you must purchase one (and for some strange reason gun-dog trainers, both amateur and professional, appear to have great difficulty in resisting the temptation to purchase all sorts of knick-knacks connected with their pursuit), use it wisely and in small doses.

One of its greatest advantages is that, if you have no rabbits, a degree of steadiness can be achieved by now and again in conjunction with the stop whistle, launching a rabbit-skin dummy low across the ground in full view of the dog and, leaving him on the drop, you walk slowly out and retrieve it yourself. This not only gives the dog a view similar to that he will have if he in the future pushes a rabbit out of the thick into the open, but will show him that not every retrieve is his.

If the dummy is pushed all the way down the spigot of the launcher, it will have maximum thrust on discharge. Launched at a 45 degree angle, the dummy will then be propelled a good 70yd. Obviously, when beginning marking lessons with a young dog, this would be a ridiculous distance to expect him to mark, go out and retrieve. Therefore in the early stages, as in all lessons, you must play safe and make the first few marked retrieves easy for the dog by only pushing the dummy approximately halfway down the spigot. Use your imagination and ingenuity in devising a variety of retrieves. You will find that the dog's ability to mark will improve with practice.

The launcher may also be utilised in the next two exercises.

First
dummy

Dog

Second
dummy

○
Handler
The two-dummies exercise

THE TWO-DUMMIES EXERCISE

As with all the other retrieving lessons, this exercise is given immediately on the dog reaching the chosen training venue. Proceed as follows: drop the dog approximately 5yd in front of you, throw one dummy to your left, keep the dog on the drop, throw another dummy out to the right, pause, then send the dog for the first dummy with a clear hand-signal. His natural reaction will always be to pursue the last dummy thrown. This must be discouraged. If the dog gets to the wrong dummy before you can stop him, do not make a fuss, just accept the dummy from him, take him back to his original drop position, collect the other dummy, go back to your position in front of the dog, and start all over again. One dummy to the left, one dummy to the right, pause, then send the dog for the first dummy thrown. If you are successful, as soon as he retrieves to hand praise him, put him back on the drop spot, back off 5yd, throw the dummy back out to the left, pause, then send the dog for the dummy to your right. Once again he will want to go for the last dummy thrown – the one to the left in this instance. Be ready to stop him and insist on his going to the right.

As with any new introduction into the training schedule, especially with a dog of a sensitive disposition, do not make a big thing of it – no more than one exercise per session, then carry on as usual. I have always found it useful to utilise the turn-whistle signal in conjunction with the left- or right-hand signal in this exercise, but do make your hand-signals clear. When watching a top-handler you will notice minimum commands and hand-signals, but they are clearly executed. There is no room for misunderstanding in the dog's mind.

As always, we are paving the way for the future. This is the embryonic stage of handling at distance ('sheep-dogging' if you like), but very necessary in a shooting dog if you want maximum efficiency in retrieving, and essential if success in field tests or field trials is envisaged.

Should any difficulty be experienced with this exercise, it may help if you start by dropping the dog in front of you, throwing one dummy out to the right, backing off to your position at 5yd distance, waiting the usual few seconds, then sending the dog with a clear hand-signal. When he becomes proficient at this you may then proceed with the two dummies. After sufficient practice with the two dummies, you increase the distance that you throw them out to right and left of the dog and, as efficiency increases with each subsequent exercise you gradually increase your own distance from the dog until you can place the dummies and then back off to a distance of 15–20yd before directing him. If you think about this, you will realise that the further you can throw the dummies, the more leeway you allow yourself to stop the dog with the stop whistle and redirect him if he has made a mistake. The procedure is always the same however. If he beats you to the punch, accept the dummy, take him back to his drop position, and throw the dummy back to its original site. Then send him for the opposite one.

This exercise gives the dog an eye-view of you handling at distance, and builds up his obedience and retrieving efficiency. If carried out first on fairly bare ground, then in rough grass as he gets more proficient and confident, no difficulty should be experienced when ultimately out shooting he is called upon to get out to a blind fall and, in conjunction with the training still to come, take a line.

There is nothing difficult in this, but it does take a fair amount of repetition to reach efficiency. As always, proceed by small doses.

THE THREE-DUMMIES EXERCISE

To complete the last exercise requires the addition of a third dummy and the go-back retrieve. When the dog is on the drop, you have just thrown out the left and right dummies. Standing in front of and facing him as usual from your 5yd position, you throw a third dummy straight out over his head. As this was the

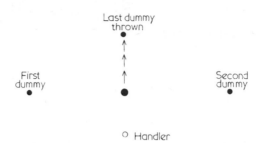

Last dummy
thrown
●

First
dummy
●

Second
dummy
●

●

○ Handler

The three-dummies exercise: to encourage confidence, initially the dog is sent for the dummy lying out behind him. Thereafter the sequence is altered periodically until proficiency is attained

last dummy thrown, it follows that you can now ring the changes with three dummies. However in the first couple of sessions with the third dummy, send the dog out on the 'Get out' command for that particular dummy (which is straight out behind him), to give him confidence. Naturally on success you then send him for one or other of the two dummies still out to his left or right, remembering of course that each time he retrieves to hand, you place him back on the original drop position before backing off and sending him for another retrieve.

Because this involves a lot of retrieving, which I do not like in hand training, at the first hint of the dog getting bored – ie slowing down, inattention, looking unhappy – call a halt to the session as far as this exercise goes. It can be returned to as a touch of variety every now and again in the normal training session. Some dogs take to this type of exercise like the proverbial duck to water, whilst others quickly lose confidence. Do not pursue this line of training in the heat of the day.

COLD GAME

Assuming that the previous exercises have been a success, and that the dog is still a keen retriever, we can progress naturally on to the next variation.

Taking a rabbit shot the day before, ie cold game, proceed in the usual manner to drop the dog, throw the dummy out to left or right, the rabbit out in the opposite direction, pause, send the dog with the usual hand and whistle signals for the dummy,

94

then straight away upon him retrieving the dummy to hand, send him for the cold rabbit with the addition of the vocal command, 'Dead'. As soon as he reaches the rabbit, give him no time to potter over it or sniff at it, get him back to you as quickly as possible. In this way he will have it back to hand without realising the difference between it and the rabbit-skin dummy.

Over the next few weeks incorporate a cold rabbit into as many sessions as possible. Always use freshly shot game, no more than 24 hours old. One rabbit, one retrieve; never, never, use the same rabbit twice. The dog will know if you do. Furthermore never use a rabbit which has been retrieved by another dog, for it will have that dog's scent on it, also, and this is just as important, make sure that the rabbit has not been badly shot, and that it has little or preferably no blood on it, for this will encourage hard mouth. With a boisterous, bold puppy, you may find that after he has delivered the rabbit the first few times, he will make a jump up for it as you are putting it away in your bag, or carrying it by your side. Discourage this by using the 'No. Leave it' command; he will soon learn – it is just the novelty of it. The first few times the dog may be reluctant to let go of the rabbit, don't let this develop into a tug-of-war; remember his mouth. You may even find that he will not release it after you have squeezed his top gums. This is unusual, but if it does happen, press firmly with your toe on his front paw. After you have done this a few times he will release it quite readily, and you should have no further problems.

Very often a young dog bites and even crushes the first few head of game he retrieves. This must not be confused with hard mouth, for in the majority of cases it is either caused by inexperience or, in the case of a sensitive puppy, anxiety. This is another very potent argument against punishing a puppy in his early days for picking up a prized object in the house; likewise punishing a dog for running away, when he comes back. These early mistakes tie in with the clenching of the teeth as he approaches you with game in his mouth in later years. In my opinion the majority of game is crushed in the last few yards because of this anxiety instilled into the dog with regard to coming back or having something in his mouth, or even to his actually having been punished whilst retrieving. As with gun-shyness, thankfully, and owing to enlightened breeding policies over the past few years, hard mouth in the hereditary sense is rare.

In the cold-game exercises, introduce birds into the training in the same way, ie throw the feather dummy out to the right of the dog, the bird out to his left, pause, send the dog for the dummy and, immediately on his delivering it, send him for the bird. On success make a great fuss of him. It is very tempting in the off-season to use pigeon in this context. Be warned, by virtue of their being loose-feathered, they tend to put a dog off retrieving because the feathers are inclined to stick in the dog's throat and mouth. They are thus distasteful, and very often a young dog will refuse to pick them in the future. There is plenty of time to introduce pigeon into his curriculum when he is older and has been out shooting a few times.

It is a simple matter to freeze game in the freezer during the shooting season to be used later in the spring and summer months for training purposes, this will be dealt with in Chapter 8.

SUMMARY

1 Do not take the puppy out solely for the purpose of giving this exercise; incorporate it in the general context of training as a variation, but never on its own.
2 This can be an extremely frustrating aspect of training, but you must not get excited, or punish the dog, nor is it desirable to show the dog your anxieties by shouting and wildly gesticulating. Have patience and all will come right in the end.
3 As some dogs do not take kindly to a lot of retrieving, you would be wise to observe your dog's attitude at all times whilst engaged in this aspect of training, and at the first sign of boredom or anxiety in the dog, abandon the exercise for a while. It can always be returned to as an added touch of variety every now and again in later training. Remember, moderation in all things.
4 Do not stare into the dogs eyes as he returns to you with the retrieve.
5 Make your signals clear, the object of this exercise is to familiarise the dog with hand signals presented to him at a distance.

CHAPTER EIGHT

Taking a Line

USING COLD GAME

Still using the cold game, as in the previous lesson, we take another step forward. Some dogs are 'naturals' when it comes to taking a line, others are not. You will find quite often that a dog that is a natural when it comes to following a runner, is also a dog that is reluctant to accept handling out to a blind retrieve. This in my view is because he possesses a very good nose which, whilst it aids him in the following of a line, tends to encourage him when part-way out to a 'blind' to branch off on the first pocket of scent he encounters and very often, in the belief that he must be right and you wrong, makes him 'whistle deaf' because of his preoccupation with foot-scent. Dogs with poorer noses, however, tend to depend more on the handler for guidance, and experience difficulty in following a line. So what we lose on the roundabouts we gain on the swings. This once again goes to prove that no two dogs are the same, and that the perfect dog is still to be born.

Nevertheless, a high degree of efficiency in all aspects of taking a line can be attained with a little patience and perseverance. It is well worth working on, for obviously if you have a dog that will handle out to the fall of an unmarked bird in the shortest possible time and then if the bird is a runner make a speedy job of the line, the greater your chances are of collecting a wounded bird and despatching it. Not only is this humanely desirable, it is also a tremendous asset in field trials.

So, if your dog picked up the handling out to a 'blind' with little or no difficulty, do not be surprised if he appears at first to be rather lacking when it comes to a line. He will develop in time. Indeed, one of the finest dogs I have ever trained and which ultimately became one of the best dogs on a runner that I have ever had is 'Macsiccar Michelle' who, from very early on could be handled on to the proverbial sixpence. Nonetheless, I had almost given up all hope of her ever becoming a useful dog on a line until one day at a trial, in her second season, she found a rabbit in thick rushes with half an inch of water underfoot. The rabbit ran through the rushes out into the open on my left, was shot at and missed, turned, ran in a straight line up the edge of the bog, turned back into the rushes about 40yd out, broke cover again away to my right, and on seeing the spectators turned back into the rushes and was shot by the right-flank gun. This happened on a cold day in late November with an east wind blowing, and thus no scent. My heart sank to my boots when the judge said, 'sorry, Joe, that's your rabbit, send your dog.' Needless to say, as I could not see her in the thick rushes where she had dropped, I could not handle her out to the rabbit so there was nothing else for it but to send her with the command 'Dead'. As I heard her splashing off through the rushes I had every expectation of a failure and inevitable disqualification. Imagine my surprise when, in less time than it takes to tell, she presented me with the rabbit. She won that trial, and from that day to this has never failed me on a runner – experience had developed her nose.

Patience, and all will come right in the end. From now on, until the puppy demonstrates to you that he is capable of taking a line, give him the following lesson periodically. It makes no matter if two or three weeks go by between. Again, don't make a ritual of it; it is better to consider this more of an opportunity to ring the changes, than to overdo it. Your dog by now should be a proficient retriever, and so from now on cut retrieving to only the occasional 'blind' or 'get out', thus you will keep him sharp and keen. You will be going on to warm, freshly shot game in the next exercise, this should be ample retrieving until you go shooting over him for real.

Meanwhile, get a piece of light cord – approximately 30ft long is sufficient. Make a small non-slip loop at one end so that by passing the cord through this loop you have a noose. It is immaterial whether you put the noose around the neck of a cold rabbit or around the waist, so long as it holds firm and does not work loose. At this juncture some authorities recommend cutting the rabbit's throat or making cuts in its legs to provide blood-scent for the dog to follow. I used to practise this doctrine myself; however, after much thought I came to the conclusion that dead game such as a rabbit does not bleed profusely enough to give off much blood-scent. Furthermore, if a bird were only 'wing-tipped', ie, two or three pellets at the most in one wing, what possible blood-scent could these few small puncture wounds produce? I concluded none at all, certainly not in the first few yards after the bird had come down, and this area of 'fall' is the most vital to the dog. For it is in the immediate vicinity of the 'fall' that the experienced dog realises (a) that it is a runner he is after, (b) what direction the game has taken. Furthermore, on many occasions I have seen a running cock, which had only a few pellets in it, collected after a long and arduous pursuit. In spite of his providing little or no blood-scent, and on land criss-crossed with foot-scent, the dog was unerring on the line. Logically then, there must be a scent-difference of some sort enabling the dog to distinguish between the wounded-bird scent and the myriad other ground-scents. And, it must be a very pungent scent, for I have seen such a bird collected even on the worst scenting days.

It seems to me that the only scent it could be is powder-scent from the hot pellets. There may be a fear-scent mingled with this, but this is debatable. It must, in fact, be obvious to anyone giving this matter even the most cursory examination, that this powder-scent is much stronger than a blood-scent ever could be for the dog to follow. Proof of this, if proof be needed, can be seen on a cold day, or even more so when the ground is wet, and a rabbit is shot. As the shot strikes the ground, all around the rabbit there is a small cloud of smoke or steam, and if you walk up to that spot, even minutes later, you can smell the powder yourself without even bending down. How much more potent must this be to a dog, whose scenting powers far exceed our own.

I have therefore come to the conclusion that to cut the rabbit's legs is purely for our own psychological benefit, but otherwise is a complete waste of time. However, if you need a psychological crutch then by all means cut the legs or throat, it will do no

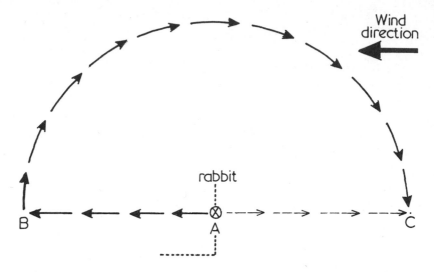

Laying a line: a rabbit is attached to a cord. The cord is paid out from *A* to *B*, then kept taut as the trainer takes a circuitous route to *C*. The rabbit is then dragged along the ground up to the trainer from *A* to *C*

harm, and perhaps there is a faint aroma of blood which will mingle with the powder-scent. However I maintain it is the latter that the dog follows.

To return to the exercise itself, various authorities stress that you should not leave your own foot-scent around the rabbit. I don't think it matters all that much to a puppy. Certainly I do not advocate leaving a foot-scent for the dog to follow, but at the start of the line I do not think it has any real bearing on the outcome. Choose a good scenting day – a dull, mild one, with damp ground and a slight breeze, is ideal. You have the rabbit attached to a cord above now, take it to the site, lay it on the ground and, holding the starter pistol against its side, fire a couple of shots. This will leave a powder-scent on the rabbit and for a few inches on the ground around it. Taking the cord, pay it out as you walk down-wind away from the rabbit. Once you have reached the end of the cord, without moving the rabbit and holding the cord at its full length, make a semi-circle until you are up-wind of the rabbit, then pull the rabbit up towards you. Detach the cord and, walking back the way you came until you

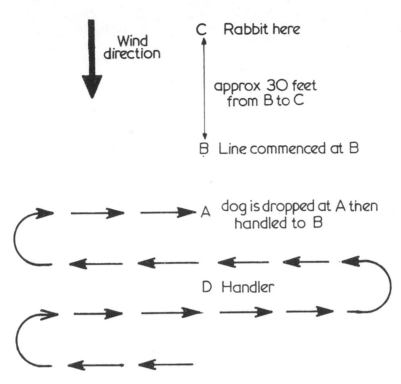

Taking a line: the dog is hunted up to *A*, he is then dropped to a shot-and-whistle command. After a pause he is given the command 'dead, get out' by the handler at *D* with the appropriate hand signal

are down-wind again from the rabbit, go and get your dog.

Start the dog hunting well down-wind of the rabbit and hunt him up to the fall (where you started the line). As he draws up to the fall, he will indicate that he is scenting something. Drop him to the whistle, and at the same time fire a shot with the starter pistol. Pause to let him gather his thoughts, then give him the command to retrieve. I do not think it necessary, with only 30ft to go, that you should tell him to get out. Neither do I think it desirable, because once a dog has his nose on a line it is better not to distract him. Whether he takes the line or just gets there, providing he retrieves the rabbit, makes no difference, for he will reach perfection with practice. This is something he has to develop in his own good time. As already said, some dogs take to it like a duck to water, others take a little longer.

Your dog by now should have had enough cold game put out for him to be quite blasé about it. This next exercise is just another progression, a step forward, albeit a transition of great importance if hard mouth is not to be induced. Take a cold rabbit, plus a rabbit shot within the last hour or so, sit the dog down in front of you, throw the cold rabbit out, pause, then send him for it. Immediately he delivers it, throw out the 'warm' rabbit, pause, then send him for it. If over the next few sessions you follow this procedure, there should be no problem. All that is left to do at this stage is to experience your dog on as wide a variety of game as possible, whenever opportunity presents itself. Obviously if you are training the dog during the summer, your choice and consequently the dog's experience, will be restricted to rabbit until the game season comes around. As mentioned earlier, I do not under any circumstances advocate the use of pigeon, although there is no harm done if you encase a freshly shot pigeon in one leg of a pair of nylon tights, and this does correspond to a certain extent to the feel and bulk of a bird. However in training many dogs over the past few years without pigeon, because of its scarcity in my area, I have substituted pheasant, duck and snipe from the freezer, plus hare. Many of these have been frozen and thawed out more than once for the purpose – needless to say they are labelled not for cooking – and I have had no trouble in the transition from the training situation to picking up on the shooting day proper.

As I believe a lot more harm than good can possibly come of using pigeons, I suggest you do not introduce the dog to them until he has had a fair amount of retrieving the real thing. If you haven't got a freezer, no matter, the humble bunny will bridge the gap until the shooting season comes along. Just remember that you introduce the dog to every new species of game in the way outlined above.

Having read a report on a field test recently where cold game from a freezer had been used, I was astounded and rather amused to note that, whilst the reporter considered this an interesting innovation, he had reservations about it as some of the dogs were reluctant to, some indeed even refused to, pick up *'half-frozen birds*'. I would have thought that it was only commonsense to make sure that the game was thoroughly thawed out before expecting a dog to retrieve it. But because there does seem misunderstanding about this, it must be emphasised that game should be thawed out properly.

SUMMARY

1 Whilst it is of no real importance whether or not you leave a foot-scent at the beginning of the 'drag-line' it is important that there is none leading to the eventual site where you wish the dog to find the rabbit.
2 As your dog becomes more proficient in following a 'line' you may increase the length by using a longer cord. Do not increase the length of the line by dragging the rabbit as you walk, for the dog will recognise your scent and follow it to the exclusion of the rabbit or powder scent, and you will defeat your purpose.
3 If on first introduction to the 'warm' rabbit your dog shows a tendency to shake it or is suspicious about it, this would indicate that you had not given him enough experience on cold game. A few more 'cold' game retrieves are necessary before trying him on warm game again. Remember, play safe at all times.
4 The game must be *thawed thoroughly* before use.

CHAPTER NINE

The End of Hand Training

STEADINESS TO GAME

This is the acid test, for in this exercise lies the proof of the pudding. If all has gone well with the hand training – training as opposed to breaking – your dog has been well and truly conditioned in good habits. I maintain that if a dog has been hand trained properly, ic he has not been allowed to see a rabbit until now, he should drop to the stop whistle at the first rabbit he flushes.

The dog's natural instinct is to hunt, chase and kill game. It is this instinct that we channel to our advantage. You should by now have instilled a high degree of obedience to the drop whistle, but as you hunt your dog you must watch him closely. Never let yourself be distracted. Do not assume that all will be well; for whilst you are wandering along expounding the virtues of your dog to a friend or discussing some other topic, that is the moment when he will find and be in full cry after game before you realise it. Consequently your training is back to square one, all because of a moment's carelessness. From now on until the end of your first shooting season you must not relax your vigilance. At no time must you lose sight of your dog. You must adhere to this code of practice until it becomes a habit – until you and your dog are an efficient hunting team.

Take your dog to the shoot or some place preferably with a liberal population of rabbits, leaving the gun at home the first few times, and hunt your dog as usual. Never mind chucking out dummies or firing blank shots, today you are only concerned with steadiness. Hunt the dog up-wind in light ground cover, ie heather, dead bracken or grass; keep him away from the gorse bushes or any other heavy cover. Remember you want him where you can see him and can keep a pattern in his ground treatment.

Watch him, he will indicate when he is working up to a find. In this split-second before he flushes blow the stop-whistle, short and sharp. It is in this split second that you must *steal the initiative* from the dog. He has dropped to the whistle at the same instant as the rabbit leaves its 'seat'. Thus, by the time he has collected his thoughts, the rabbit should be well and truly on the way home. Now the instant you have dropped the dog, it is perfectly in order, indeed desirable the first few times, to endorse it with a low but firm vocal 'Hup', repeated if necessary once or twice until the rabbit is out of view. Weather conditions will determine the duration of each hunt. Obviously if it is a hot day it will be a short session, with a correspondingly longer one on a cold day. Never hunt a dog on unproductive ground, if there is no game about and no scent, call it a day and go home. It is a well known fact that, for some unknown reason, rabbits sit better in the morning and get more flighty as the day progresses. Naturally then, it is desirable to conduct the early training sessions as far as possible during the morning. In this way your dog will get maximum finds whereas, hunted in the afternoon or evenings, the ground game will tend to get up on hearing your approach, your dog will only find hot 'seats', and will get minimum opportunity to flush. Should your young dog break at the flush of a rabbit, get after him, take him back by the scruff to the exact 'seat', push his nose into it, flap back his ear and blast the stop-whistle into it, alternating with the vocal command, 'There'. 'Hup'. He will, if you are consistent in this, learn by telling in the end. And learn he must, for just as in retrieving, where a dog who will not come to hand naturally will not deliver a retrieve to hand, if the dog will not drop to the drop-whistle, every time without exception, then he will most definitely not drop in a 'hot-corner'. The training of dogs, after all is said and done, is only commonsense tempered with patience; if you rush it, you will pay the price.

If you have been successful, and there should be no excuse for failure if you have done the groundwork properly, praise the dog, then hunt him on *in the opposite direction to that the rabbit has taken*. By this I do not mean you alter your direction from that in which you were hunting the dog before the flush, but that you *cast the dog off* in the opposite direction, and hunt on as before. Some dogs will accept this without question, others will tend to want to 'line' after the rabbit the first few times. It is a great help if you introduce the command 'Gone away' as you cast the dog off after each flush. It also helps if you endorse it with the command familiar by now, 'Leave it'.

Continue in this manner for the first few sessions. Remember, no gun, and do *give the dog time to work his beat.* Do not walk over him, far too many shooters take up ground far too fast, as though they were on a route march. Nothing destroys a dog's pattern faster than this; take your time, you will find more game that way and, after all, that is the object of the exercise.

The question of punishment has already been discussed but, now that your dog's hand training is at an end, it seems useful to stress again one or two points particularly relevant to steadiness. Although the majority of dogs will get the message by the methods outlined there are some dogs who, by virtue of their temperamental deficiencies due to faulty breeding ie – excitability and unwillingness to please – demand sterner measures. But be careful, by now you should know your puppy very well, and can judge whether he is excitable and possibly sensitive with it. If so you have a difficult choice, for if you resort to physical punishment you may stop him hunting altogether, and in all probability destroy his trust to such an extent that you will never attain the same degree of rapport with him again.

Remember, a dog learns from association. Let us assume that we have a dog who is very sensitive – probably he is very intelligent as well, this kind usually are – and you have him out hunting for the first time. He finds a rabbit and gives chase, probably due to your being slow with the whistle, and once a dog is in full cry after a rabbit it is extremely difficult to stop him. You must be honest with yourself, were you too slow? In that case it is your fault, not the dog's. So simply get hold of him when he comes back, say nothing, take him by the scruff back to the rabbit's 'seat', flap back his ear and blow the stop whistle in it a couple of times as described earlier. With a sensitive dog this is sufficient.

Incorporate a rabbit into as many sessions as possible

As his confidence grows with experience in water, you will be able to handle him with whistles together with the appropriate hand signals

Field-trial winner Macsiccar Michele, the most consistent trial dog I have ever owned

Your friend's shooting for you will enable you to give much more attention to your dog

Through their respective owners' anxiety in relation to steadiness, many dogs have been completely put off hunting because they have been severely dealt with on the first few occasions that they have met with the rabbit. They begin to associate the scent with the rabbit and the inevitable hiding. Once a dog has been abreacted in this fashion, you will have a devil of a job to get him going again, indeed, it may be impossible. Therefore, tread warily, be sure of your dog's temperament. If he has illustrated to you in the past that he has a sensitive streak, gently does it.

On the other hand however, if your dog has shown you in past sessions that he has a bloody-minded streak and that he is a tough-nut then, provided you were not too slow with the whistle and that you are certain it is not your fault, in other words he has deliberately defied you, get after him, drag him back to the rabbit's 'seat', blast the stop-whistle over and over in his ear, shove his nose into the 'seat' repeating over and over again, 'There'. 'Hup'. 'There'. 'Hup', and give him a sharp lesson on the rump with the flat of your hand. Do not lose your temper, if punishment is to be employed it must be administered with a cool clear head. If you lose your temper with a dog in any situation, it will invariably cause more work for you at the end of the day.

Under no circumstances use a stick or boot. If you have to resort to such cruelty, far better resign yourself to being dogless, for neither you nor the unfortunate animal will ever be happy in each other's company. It may be my imagination, but this kind of treatment appears to have increased over the past few years. However, if you have to resort to what after all can only be described as extreme measures, do make sure that the lesson goes home. Do not adopt a namby-pamby approach, for with this type of temperament, it is very easy to case-harden a dog by continually being 'on' at him, giving him a slap, gradually getting harder and harder, so that the dog builds up a resistance to such an extent that he could withstand the severest and most bestial approach and consequently be utterly useless. One sharp lesson is kindness to the dog, continually increasing pressure is cruelty.

I think by now I should have made myself perfectly clear.

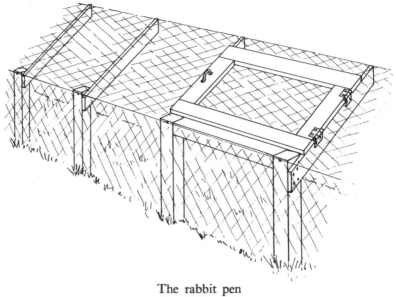

The rabbit pen

The average dog will train to a high degree without a finger laid on him, but occasionally if you are unlucky you will encounter a dog possessed. When the necessity arises this type of dog should, in one swift lesson, be shown a glimpse of hell. In this way one lesson should be adequate.

THE RABBIT PEN

The rabbit pen can be a great asset to the steadying of a dog; it is an essential part of the professional trainer's equipment, as he has so many dogs to steady and demonstrate for his clients. However, as this book is intended for the amateur trainer, I feel that because of its temptations and consequent drawbacks it is an expensive and unnecessary luxury. For instance, it is very tempting in the one- or two-dog situation to be continually hunting them in the pen, with the result that the dogs get into the habit of sight-hunting. That is to say they get used to looking for the quarry to the exclusion of hunting for it with their noses.

Furthermore, a dog that has any brains at all will soon be educated to the pen, and far from steadying him to rabbits it will, in many cases, have the opposite effect, ie he will drop to the flush in the pen, but once outside it and involved in hunting proper will realise that he is free, and chase. Over-indulgence in hunting a dog in a pen will result in the dog being hesitant and having no fluent hunting pattern. I stress here of course that I am talking of extreme cases.

For those who are still interested in constructing a rabbit pen, and are not too clear as to how to go about it, here are a few tips. The smallest area worthwhile for this purpose would be approximately 400sq yd. Chicken-wire stapled to ordinary fence-posts is quite adequate for the perimeter, but a further 2ft at least must be added all the way round at the top and turned inwards at an angle of 45 degrees, to prevent the rabbits from climbing or jumping out. By far the biggest problem, especially with a small pen, is stopping the rabbit from burrowing out. Many authorities advocate the use of corrugated iron sheets sunk into the ground all the way round the pen, however costs, not to mention the amount of hard work involved in digging a 3ft-deep trench are prohibitive. I have found that a full width of chicken-wire laid flat on the ground and clipped to the bottom edge of the fence wire every few inches, more than adequately prevents any escape of the inmates. It is advisable to weight the wire down with large stones until the grass has grown up through the mesh. With this type of fence, all that is required for a gate is a 'flap over' of the turned-in wire at the top, thus there will be no joints or gaps in the actual fence.

A pen of these proportions cannot support a large population, nevertheless it should be quite adequate for the spare-time trainer. Bundles of forest brashings placed at strategic points in the pen will afford cover and shade. In hot weather a supply of clean drinking water should always be available. Rabbits are not copious drinkers as a rule, getting adequate moisture from grass in the morning dew, but in extreme conditions are thankful for the extra supply. As the drinking bowls tend to get fouled by their droppings in a very short time, a regular check is essential. In taking on any type of livestock, one inherits responsibility. The humble rabbit if imprisoned needs looking after, especially in winter, when a regular supply of turnips should be left for him – four rabbits will eat one turnip nightly.

111

A rabbit pen, its construction, maintenance, and last but by no means least its inhabitants, measure up to a not inconsiderable expense and amount of work. Therefore serious thought should be given as to the necessity of owning one, especially if the training of one or perhaps two dogs at most is envisaged. In stocking a pen some authorities recommend the use of tame rabbits. I personally have never had any success in this, as the tame rabbit is reluctant to bolt and when he does it is more of a hop, skip and a jump, stopping a few yards away, usually in full view of the pup, all very frustrating both for the trainer and the dog. Without a doubt the wild rabbit is by far the better proposition, these are easily procured with the aid of a ferret and a few purse nets. As they bolt put them into a sack, they will stay there provided you keep the sack beside you; however turn your back even for a second, and they will slice through the sack and be gone in a trice. Transporting them home is no problem as the motion of the car will keep them from trying to escape.

If you have access to a friend's rabbit pen, then by all means have a go in it, but as soon as the dog has got the hang of dropping to the flush, don't take him back into the pen. Your dog may at some time or other forget his training and give chase. The advantage of a pen in this situation is that you can manufacture the event all over again the next day and in the pen it is much easier to catch him in the act. By all means make use of a pen in this instance, but refrain from overdoing pen-work.

If your dog has been trained to observe the lessons in this book up to now, you should be perfectly capable of training him to be steady in the natural way, in the open. Do not, at any time, fall into the trap of mistaking natural flair and style for 'hardness' in a dog. Always make sure you know your dog, for in this rests the ultimate success or failure of your training programme.

It may be that you do not have access to ground which has ground game on it. This is the position I was in when I first embarked on the training of gun dogs. However, don't despair, by using your initiative and ingenuity a great deal can be done to alleviate this problem, although unfortunately it entails a little

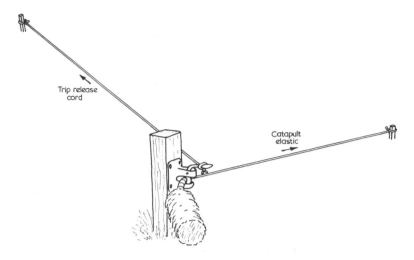

The bolting rabbit

extra work. A 'bolting' rabbit situation can be quite easily simulated by the use of a length of catapult elastic approximately 15ft long, a gate latch and a post. Attach one end of the elastic to a peg hammered into the ground, and the other end to a rabbit-skin dummy, preferably with a fresh skin on it. The elastic is then stretched to its maximum length and clicked into a gate-latch attached to another post hammered into the ground. A release cord is then attached to the gate-latch, and at a suitable distance pegged into the ground (see above). It helps if you trail a cold rabbit around, criss-crossing the ground which is to be hunted by the young dog in the vicinity of the dummy rabbit. Three or four of these devices, distributed at strategic points on the training ground, whilst they are no substitute for the real thing, will go a long way towards steadying the young dog.

The ubiquitous dummy launcher can also be utilised for steadying purposes as mentioned in Chapter 7, ie by launching a rabbit-skin dummy whilst the dog is hunting ahead of him low along the ground. The dog on hearing the report will see the tumbling dummy, which bears a striking resemblance to a toppled rabbit in the shooting situation proper. Care must be taken that in launching the dummy into the vicinity of the dog, you do not hit him with it. This is an extremely dangerous weapon, and if

Dizzying a pigeon

a dog were struck by the dummy a serious injury could be inflicted.

Throughout the book I have stressed the importance of steadying your dog to ground game for the very simple reason that a dog that will stop on ground game will stop to birds, for he knows full well that he cannot catch a flying bird. Once again we can credit the dog with some sense. Nevertheless, some practice on flushing birds can be given artificially by using the technique known as 'dizzying a pigeon'. This entails the keeping of more livestock, ie pigeon in a coop; therefore you have to ask yourself if it is worth the extra work entailed. Should you decide that you wish to embark upon it, this is how to go about it.

Take a pigeon in both hands, tuck his head under his wing and hold it gently but firmly in this fashion, rocking him with a circular motion for approximately one to two minutes. Make a 'seat' in the grass and place the pigeon in it, arranging the grass around and over him, then go and get your dog. The bird will remain in his 'seat' for about 10 minutes, therefore you have plenty of time. Hunt your dog as you normally would, and as he approaches the bird and indicates, stop whistle short and sharp on the flush. The pigeon will fly home quite unharmed by his experience. It is truly remarkable the degree of steadiness which can be attained in the artificial situation, providing a little application is exercised.

In years gone by, I have had such difficulty in procuring shooting, that I could not obtain game for the training of my puppies and had to buy the occasional bird from the game dealer. Indeed I have even used road-casualties which had not been badly mutilated for this purpose. Necessity is the mother of invention.

WALKING TO HEEL

I am not a great believer in teaching a hunting dog to walk to heel, certainly I would not consider teaching him to walk to heel prior to training him to hunt. However, in the one-man, one-dog situation where the dog may be taken shopping or to the office etc, it is certainly essential that the dog does not wander whilst off the lead. There are also situations in the shooting sphere where it is desirable that he should be reasonably controllable off the lead at heel. Nevertheless, no matter how good a standard is obtained, it must be borne in mind that it is against the law for a dog to be off the lead at anytime in a built-up area. Remember, he is your responsibility at all times.

Except in the most extreme cases it is a very simple job to train a dog to be well-behaved at heel. Put the dog on the lead as you would normally do when taking him out for a training session – the rope lead, slip type, is ideal for this purpose. Walking the dog on your left side, as he pulls ahead give him a short sharp tug back into heel saying sharply, 'Heel'. Do not engage into long-drawn-out pulls, as this will just develop into a tug-of-war and you will achieve nothing. You must make it short and sharp, and each and every time he works his way forward, repeat the treatment over and over again. Be consistent, from now on when he is on the lead this is the format. Never again must you allow him to pull or wander on the lead. Make the lesson on the lead short, about 10 minutes per day is sufficient. At the end of this short walk, let him off for some free running exercise, or by all means give him a short hunt, putting him back on the lead to be taken back home. If you do this regularly you will find that he will grasp it quite rapidly and will walk quite happily at heel or on the lead.

You will find with some dogs, especially the sensitive ones, that after having a few short hard tugs on the lead they will show their displeasure by hanging back on the lead behind you. The remedy is the same as that when they pull forward – a short, sharp pull on the lead and the command, 'Heel'. It also helps if you pat your thigh as you give the command. As time goes on the dog will associate the pat on the thigh with walking to heel.

When he has reached a good standard of heel-keeping on the lead, you can take it a step further, as you are walking along with him at heel on the lead, by lightly letting go of the lead and laying it gently along his back. Continue walking as you do this, for you do not want to draw his attention to the fact that you are not holding the lead anymore. He may not be aware for a few seconds that anything has changed, but sooner or later he will be. He may then try to reach round and mouth the lead or knock it off his back; it will probably fall off anyway, but this is of no consequence. As soon as the dog slackens his pace or tries to walk on ahead of you, slap your thigh and say, 'Heel'. If he does not comply; take the lead and give him a really sharp tug repeating, 'Heel. Heel'. You continue in this manner in all future sessions until he gets the message, however a dog grasps this very swiftly as a rule.

The third stage, as in all other exercises, is just the extension of the previous one. Walk the dog on the lead for a little while, then snake the lead along his back as before. Continue for a little while longer, finally sit him down, take the lead off, slap your thigh, say, 'Heel', and walk on repeating every now and again, 'Good boy. Heel'. If at any time he breaks from heel, call him back with the whistle and put him back on the lead. To rebuke him, give him quite a few sharp tugs on the lead really hard, repeating in a grim voice, 'Heel. Heel.'

You should not have much difficulty with this lesson, most dogs learn what is required fairly rapidly. However bear in mind that a hunting dog may never attain perfection off the lead. Don't make a mountain out of a molehill, provided he is at heel within a yard either side of you I consider that fair enough. I would far rather have a dog that did this and was a hunter, than a dog who was perfect at heel and otherwise hopeless.

SUMMARY

1 Until now you have been conditioning your dog to respond in a desired way to your whistle signals. Taking him into the situation where he finds game for the first time is 'the acid test'. If you have been diligent with in training him and avoiding dangerous situations it is now that you will benefit.

2 If you cultivate the habit of being dog-conscious over the first few outings and maintaining vigilance at all times, you should be able to maintain a high standard of steadiness in your dog.

3 Never trust him out of your sight. Remember he is young and should the exuberance of youth and the excitement of the moment induce him to give chase, it will be even more difficult to regain a high degree of steadiness afterwards.

4 He has been taught to hunt in front of you so allow him time to cover his beat, otherwise to remain in front he has to break his hunting pattern and is therefore more likely to miss game.

5 Hunting a young inexperienced dog on unproductive ground will take the drive out of him, and you may well wind up with a lifeless potterer.

CHAPTER TEN

First Season's Experience

Now that the big day has arrived – the day that all your hard work has been for – you are at last ready to shoot over your young dog. More important, if all has gone well up to now, your dog is ready for it.

There is an old adage concerning the training of dogs which is, 'never trust a young dog'. This means simply, don't let him out of your sight at any time, never assume that he will behave himself. No matter how well you think you have trained him, he is a young dog and will succumb to the excitement of the moment very easily; he requires control at all times. If all your hard work and dedication is not to go by the board as a result of careless handling you must be attentive, concentrating on him. For the first season you must be a dog-man first and a shooting-man second. In other words, when the dog flushes game, before taking a shot, you must make sure at all times that the dog is down and staying down. Remember, you can always get another pheasant, a good dog is an entirely different matter.

To assist you in concentrating on the handling of your dog, it is a good plan to enlist the help of a friend, preferably a friend who does not possess a dog, or one who is willing to leave his dog at home to do the shooting for you. As an added safeguard to prevent yourself succumbing to the excitement of the moment and taking a pot-shot in a hot corner, thus diverting your attention for a moment from the job in hand, you should leave your own gun at home. The better the shot your friend is, the more your dog will respond and blossom, for there is no worse training than continually missing over a novice dog, and believe me it is very easy indeed to miss when you are anxious to get a retrieve.

Your friend's shooting for you will enable you to give that

much more attention to your dog. It will also help your dog to get used to the idea of other people shooting. After the first few outings, your friend can bring his own dog along and hunt it in company with yours. The effect another dog can have on a sensitive animal can be quite dramatic, so don't be surprised if your dog shows reluctance to hunt in the close proximity of another animal. However this is nothing to worry about, usually after the first few minutes he will get over the novelty of it and get on with the job. It all adds to experience – another hurdle to surmount.

However, a word of warning: choose your shooting companion carefully, paying special consideration to the dog he possesses. If it is a wild uncontrollable brute, or your friend is prone to shouting at it or worse, then it would be wise to consider someone else as your shooting partner, at least until your dog is over his first season. Remember, from your dog's view point that other dog chasing that hare is having all the fun. As with a naughty child, it's fun to be bad, therefore, your dog will quickly pick up the other dog's flair for crime. We go back to the original theme here; avoid the potentially dangerous situation.

Furthermore, if you ask your friend to go shooting with you the first few times without his dog, he will probably accept it and understand your reason, but sooner or later he is going to suggest bringing his 'Fido' along, and if you refuse then you have lost a friend. It is very strange but nevertheless true, you may criticise a friend's car, his prowess with a gun, even his girlfriend, and he will accept it in a jocular vein. But should a hint of criticism be directed at his dog you will again have lost a friend. Far better not to ask him to shoot for you at all until such times as you are confident that you have gained complete control and can maintain it, than to expect him to leave his own dog at home for ever and a day. Even the best of friends would take this as a personal slight. However, let us assume that you have solved this one and that you are out shooting at last with your protégé.

Take the lead off your dog, 'hup' him, and keep him thus for a couple of minutes. This is a lesson in obedience, and if field trials are your ultimate goal it is mandatory. Make a slow job of putting the lead into your pocket, load the gun, pause, cast

119

him off – every time you begin proceedings in this fashion in the future, you will gradually bed in another good habit. Keep your eye on the dog at all times when you are hunting him, remember you are a dog-man first and a shooting-man second. If necessary, keep an even flow of hunting pattern in him with the aid of the turn-recall whistle. If you find difficulty in working a dog on two whistles whilst carrying a gun, I know I do, wrap the whistle-lanyard around the left hand, if you are right-handed. You will find with a little practice that you can give the whistle command required with the minimum of fumbling and still have plenty of time to take a shot.

During the first season keep the dog working close to you. Remember also only to give a whistle signal when it is necessary, when it is apparent he requires it because it looks as though he is not going to turn or perhaps starts to pull out in front on a foot-scent. However, in saying that, let me emphasise never to take a chance with him the first season on the drop whistle. Use it always on a flush and make sure he is down, and staying down, before you take a shot. Never presume that he will be steady, it requires practice, you must work at it. If all goes well take your shot then, hit or a miss, immediately turn your eye on the dog and command, 'Hup'. Keep him down for a second or two whilst you unload the spent cartridge and reload, then send the dog. If you make this standard practice, it maintains steadiness and also drives home to the dog that he only goes when and if he is told.

EXPERIENCE ON RUNNERS

What if the game comes down and is a runner? The answer is to put another shot into it. The reason I say this is because we are working with a young, inexperienced dog, we wish to maintain steadiness, and at the same time there is danger in sending a young pupil for a runner, especially if he is an old cock, a hare, or a mallard drake. The first may spur him, the second may kick him, and the third may give him a nasty tweak on the end of his nose. Any of these mishaps occurring to your dog during the first season can put him off retrieving for life, especially if he has a sensitive streak. In a bolder dog it can lead to hard mouth because, when he encounters wounded game in the future, he may give it a quick squeeze to prevent retaliation. It is also a primary factor in causing a dog to 'blink' game, that is to say show hesitance to the flush or complete refusal to push game out.

But experience on runners is required therefore, as in all other aspects of training, you have to try and strike a happy medium. If possible, after he has been out shooting with you a few times try him on a running hen pheasant, and if he makes a good job of it next time try him on a wounded rabbit. You may find that if on his first encounter with a wounded rabbit it squeals as he approaches, he may turn away in alarm or uncertainty. However if you encourage him similarly to when he was a puppy on his first dummy, you will find that the majority of dogs will return to the rabbit and deliver to you. Failing this, I usually recall the dog and, giving him a reassuring pat, put another shot into the rabbit, sending the dog for it immediately. I have found that this is almost certain to solve the problem as almost invariably, on being sent for the next wounded rabbit, the dog shows no hesitation in picking it up.

Once again, moderation in all things – not too many wounded rabbits the first season, as they can give a kick. Should your dog come through this introduction with flying colours, he should have no reservation about runners in the future.

It is very important that when wounded game comes down in the open, you always wait until it reaches the cover before sending the dog for it, if steadiness is to be maintained. Never, never, send a dog for running game whilst it is still in view. For if you think about it, this is a direct contradiction to your training on steadiness, you are asking the dog to chase moving game, and this is another good reason for not giving a young dog too many runners in his first season.

Another very important word of warning is that it is common practice on a shoot for half a dozen dogs to go running in after birds down. Under no circumstances involve your dog in these free-for-alls. In the first place, if the bird is a runner, the ground will quickly become fouled by the dogs' foot-scents to such a degree that successful collection of the bird is extremely remote; only a wide-ranging, experienced dog will stand any chance whatever of picking up the line. It is now that we

121

encounter the man who, probably through laziness and/or being too mean to have his dog trained, brings his wild uncontrollable pest, a canine honours graduate in the school of experience but having only the most rudimentary of training if any – a dog who hunts in the next parish for most of the day until he is so tired he almost becomes manageable in the last half hour.

This is the dog who will very often collect the runner, probably bringing it back dead and mutilated, although for the rest of the day we are subjected to the owner's derisory comments about the shortcomings of our young inexperienced dog and the virtues of his. This kind of owner is best ignored. It is this type of fool who will telephone a professional kennel expecting a fully trained dog within a month. On numerous occasions I have answered the 'phone to be told, 'I am going on holiday for a month and thought it would be a jolly good opportunity to have the dog trained, and I can pick him up on the way home.' It takes all kinds!

Should you be unfortunate enough to share a shoot with this type of gentleman, and should you be fortunate enough to get the chance of a retrieve, look around to see if there is a dog down on it. Is there likely to be one sent for it? Have the other dog-owners seen it down? If the answer is no, then quietly send your young dog. I say quietly, because it is truly amazing the number of people who, whilst they consider themselves your friend will, on seeing a promising young dog down after a bird, send their dog, even if they see that yours is actually in the act of picking the bird. There is little you can do in this situation other than, if your dog has not reached the bird, stop him with the stop whistle and call him back as soon as you see the dangerous situation developing.

The only advice I can give you is, if you think your shoot has dogs and owners like this, go shooting on your own, for a young dog will be quickly ruined in such a situation. This one upmanship, for that is what it is, quickly leads to a young dog becoming hard mouthed, because in the multi-dog tournament for a bird it is snatched first from one dog's mouth to another's thus teaching the dogs to grip. To repeat, stay away from this situation. As time goes on your dog will get his fair share of retrieves and, what is more important, benefit from them.

Let us return to shooting over the dog yourself, or at most in the company of a friend. Remember, after each retrieve praise the dog, drop him in front of you, pause, cast him off once more. Keep him working close. In the first season I tend to keep him very tight, about 5yd to either side of me, and the same distance in front; but do not hassle the dog, let him work his ground. Give him the time to decide for himself whether he is working on to an empty 'seat' or not, before giving him the 'Gone away. Leave it' command. If he is going to turn, don't blow the whistle just for the sake of it, for as outlined earlier, unnecessary whistle commands tend to make a dog whistle-deaf.

Whilst quartering a dog, I have developed a habit of snapping my fingers. This I have found very useful, as my dogs will turn to this alone after a very short time. It makes for less noise and saves me from continually giving a whistle signal if the dog requires a lot of handling.

During a dog's first season, and whenever a new season commences, I collect the dead game myself, giving the dog perhaps one retrieve in three. In this way the idea is cemented into the dog's head that every head of game is not for him. Thus it keeps him steady to shot and fall, nothing will unsteady a dog to this faster than being sent for everything shot. It is pointless to send a young dog for a dead rabbit or bird lying out in the open, for it is dead, it isn't going anywhere. So leave the dog on the drop, walk out and collect it yourself.

Try to give the dog experience on as wide a variety of terrain and game as possible. Bear in mind always that, no matter how good you think he is, out of sight he may be a little devil. So keep him in sight at all times. This is difficult in, for instance, gorse bushes. A young dog is very much inclined to pull out in front of you in this type of cover, especially if game is running on ahead. Likewise rhododendrons hold scent and tend to 'hot' a young dog up, consequently in this type of cover or any other where the dog is obscured from your view, be on your guard, keep on top of him, use your recall whistle to keep in touch with him and, as he reappears, swing him back into the cover at your feet. In this type of terrain you will have to use your ears as much as your eyes. You will soon learn to differentiate between him bustling through the cover and the sudden upsurge of sound and activity as he pushes game. Use your stop whistle, pause, if nothing appears, 'Good boy'. 'Gone away'. Immediately recall him, get him back to you, and once again put him into the cover at your feet, this prevents the temptation to line out in the direction that the game has taken.

I should make it clear at this point that, when a young dog 'hots up' and lines out he will, in all probability, be 'deaf' to the recall whistles. Therefore always drop him with the drop whistle, pause, then use the recall whistle; if your hand training has been bedded in properly, the stop whistle should be the ultimate deterrent. A dog worked in this fashion in thick cover will soon become very proficient at pushing game and dropping by himself, but he's young, so continue to use the drop whistle. Remember, take no chances in the first season.

A habit which must be nipped in the bud is 'pegging'. This is when a dog, usually a very keen hunter, instead of trying to flush the game, catches it in its 'seat'. This is unfortunate, for not only will it preclude you getting a shot, it will invariably lead to the dog killing game, thus instilling hard mouth. Whether your aim is field trials or not, jump on this habit straight away. Leave him in no doubt as to your views on this, if acted on from the moment of the initial crime it is usually sufficient to order him with 'Leave it.' If he persists, you must adopt sterner measures, and you must persist until you have cured him. At all costs it must be stopped; it helps, but does not solve the problem, if you are a little quicker with the stop whistle. But there is a danger here too, for if you are too quick with the whistle you may stop the dog short of the flush and, if done too often, this will tend to take away the panache and drive as he rushes in to flush game.

I personally like a dog who is positive in the flush, and dislike one that points before the flush, however there are many who like the added refinement of a dog that points. In my opinion it is a waste of time, as it can lead to a dog pointing and indicating empty 'seats'. As far as I am concerned the dog should get on with the work in hand, which is to find and flush game to the 'gun'.

Swing him back into the cover at your feet

Wrap the whistle lanyard around the left hand

If your dog works his ground methodically at a good pace, he is probably up to trial standard

Field-trial spectators

Hunting a hard-going dog on ground where rabbits have myxomatosis will encourage a dog to 'peg' because the infected rabbit is blind or, if in the early stages of this foul disease, his senses are dulled. Such rabbits are lethargic, and consequently reluctant to bolt, allowing the dog those crucial added seconds which give him the chance to catch instead of flushing the game.

The procedure for working ditches and hedges is similar to that of working the dog in thick cover. The dog will be inclined to pull out ahead; use the recall whistle to keep him in. Very often in a ditch or hedge you will see the game running on ahead of you, don't get excited, continue at a normal pace, and on giving the dog the recall whistle always stand still, making him come back to you. The game will tuck in at the end of the cover and your dog will get the opportunity of flushing it.

Rushes also tend to hold scent resulting in a young dog 'hotting up'. Young dogs will go like the proverbial bomb in this kind of cover, and tend to pull out ahead as game runs on ahead of you. The handling technique is the same: call the dog back with the recall whistle, stand still, and as he approaches you swing him off to the right or left. Keep him quartering, if you do not proceed forward until the dog is back to you and you have cast him off to the right or left, he will get the idea of not boring on ahead – consistency is the keynote. The ideal cover for spaniels to work in a good pattern is dead bracken, heather and light rushes.

Do not at any time wander across meadows or any other bare ground with the spaniel at the loose whilst you chat to your friends. Never waste your dog's time by hunting him on bare unproductive ground, for this will teach him to range on ahead and, if you bring pressure to bear in an effort to work him close, he will ultimately slow down and develop into a potterer. Put your dog on a lead when crossing bare ground.

Always drop your dog before you get over an obstacle and, leaving him on the drop until you are over, call him to you when you are in control of the situation, and drop him again momentarily once he is over. This also instills obedience in him.

Giving tongue, like 'pegging', is another habit which can very often be prevented if dealt with the first time it occurs. But here, however, I am speaking in the context of a dog out shooting, not a young puppy. If your dog is old enough to go shooting, then he should be past the age of puppy exuberance when he will give an excited yelp for the sheer hell of it. Consequently, if you hear him give tongue, quickly command him, 'No', drop him, go up to him and give him a sharp rebuke, accompanied by, 'Be quiet. No. Be quiet'. Offer up a prayer that this habit is not inherent, for if it is you will either have to live with it or get rid of the dog.

In saying that, however, do not be too despondent, for there is a market for a well trained, steady dog, and there are shooters who could not care less whether he gives tongue or not. But before selling him, you must be honest and tell the prospective client exactly why you are parting with him. Under no circumstances should a dog like this be bred from, therefore before selling him it is your duty to the breed to register him at the Kennel Club as not to be bred from.

Should you be fortunate enough to have a friend who possesses a good dog, it is a good plan to shoot a rabbit that your dog has found and, whilst you keep your dog on the drop, your friend sends his dog past yours to the retrieve. Conversely, when your friend's dog finds a rabbit, you send your dog past his for it. This is a marvellous way of instilling a high degree of steadiness and if field trials are your aim it is an essential exercise as this happens all the time in a trial. The line is stopped as one dog is sent for a retrieve, and more often than not your dog can see all that is going on. It is a great temptation for a young dog to throw caution to the winds and go charging out.

In a field trial there is nothing you can do about it other than to put your lead on when the dog returns, for you are out of the stake. However should it happen whilst out shooting, get after him quickly, drag him back to his original drop position, scold him and blast the stop whistle in his ear. He will soon learn, for it is just the recklessness of youth. Needless to say, should he reach the game before you intercept him, you must accept the retrieve with the minimum of fuss. There is nothing you can do about it, for you have lost the initiative, you cannot punish him either by word or deed; time enough the next time.

If your dog is of a sensitive disposition, you have to be doubly careful in your choice of partner for your dogging forays for, if your friend be a 'hard' trainer and he punishes his dog in view of your young dog, this can have a very serious effect indeed on him, even to the point of his refusing to hunt, for dogs seeing another dog being punished take it personally.

Occasionally someone tells me that after the first outing with the gun their dog, which until then had been doing very well, developed the habit of not hunting, tending to fall into heel when the gun is carried. When asked what the dog is like when the owner is not carrying a gun, the reply usually is that he hunts all right. This is a late manifestation of gun-nervousness, and in nine cases out of ten the shot exercises have been skimped. I include this at this point more as a precaution for, if you have followed the lessons outlined in this book correctly, it should not happen. However as all dogs, not to mention people, are different, it is possible. Immediately you notice even a wariness come over the dog, resist shooting over him, for his tendency demands remedial attention straight away. The only solution is to return to the shot exercises and give a course of revision.

A dog's performance in the shooting field may vary greatly from day to day, depending on the prevailing weather conditions. On a day when scent is bad he will tend to hunt much slower than usual, whereas on a good scenting day he will go like a bomb. On a windy day a dog who normally is very obedient and at one with his handler may display a different side to his character; generally speaking, gale force winds have an adverse effect on a dog, so in these conditions expect the worst.

As this book is geared to the ordinary shooting-man's require- ments, in all probability many of its readers will not be over endowed with shooting facilities. If they possess ground at all, or rent a small shoot, the game supply may not be all that plentiful, yet it is desirable to put up sufficient game in the first few outings to keep your young dog keen. Many small shoots carry a sufficient population of rabbits for this, however, after the first few shots especially, the population go to ground. This can be alleviated to a great extent by what is known as 'stinking out'. Whilst this procedure is not all that well known, it can be very effective, and a shoot which normally may produce half a dozen rabbits in a day can show a dramatic increase in the bag if it is done properly. The only materials required are discarded diesel oil mixed with Reynardine. Newspaper is torn up into strips and soaked in this mixture, which is certainly the most effective one to use. However any strong-smelling liquid like creosote or strong disinfectant will serve the same purpose. If, four or five days before your intended shooting day, a piece of the treated newspaper is placed to arm's length in each burrow, leaving perhaps two burrows clear for exit routes, you will find on your shooting day that the residents have left the burrows and are tightly tucked in out in the open. This should afford your dog many more finds than he would normally get.

It is important that you give four to five clear days interval before the intended shooting day, because the smell not only takes time to pervade the whole burrow system but has the effect of keeping the bunnies at home for the first two or three days before they evacuate the burrow.

SUMMARY

1 Never trust a young dog; out of sight he will succumb to temptation . . . *concentrate.*
2 Whilst the basic training is by far the most important, the first season's experience is also very important. It is the 'icing on the cake'.
3 At all times avoid dangerous situations and play safe.
4 Always allow running game to reach cover before sending your dog for it, otherwise his steadiness will suffer in the future.
5 Never allow him to enter the multi-dog mêlée on a runner.
6 Use your whistles only if necessary.
7 Never hunt bare unproductive ground: put the lead on instead.
8 Drop him before and after an obstacle. Make it a habit.
9 *Never ever allow your dog to retrieve game which another dog has had in his mouth,* for if that dog has damaged the game it will encourage your dog to do the same, thus inducing 'hard mouth'. If a judge at a field trial asks you to send your dog for game which another dog has spat out, refuse. *You are entitled to* and he is only showing his ignorance in asking you. *He cannot penalise you* for refusing it, but make it clear to him just why you have refused.

130

CHAPTER ELEVEN

Advanced Field Technique

PICKING UP

Picking up is an invaluable way of giving a young dog experience in the field. Indeed much can be learnt in a very short time in this way; however, as in all things, there are pitfalls.

It is not all that easy to procure picking up. First of all you have to contact your local keeper. As there will be an abundance of dogs in his area – most of them with cardinal faults such as running in, hard mouth, giving tongue etc – whose owners are also looking for a day's beating or picking up, the keeper is often inundated with offers of help on his shooting days from dog owners all of whom will tell him that their particular dog is a paragon of virtue. He knows from experience to tread warily in his selection of helpers. Therefore, if he does not know you personally, he will be reluctant to give you a chance unless you can get some mutual friend or acquaintance to recommend you and your dog.

Once this hurdle is over and you get a day, remember that you are on trial. Therefore do as you are told, go to your exact station and stay there, and keep the noise to a minimum whilst moving from beat to beat. The keeper has to present the maximum birds over the 'guns' and will not take kindly to any garrulous beater who alarms the birds prematurely. If a 'gun' should be shooting badly, you would do well to keep your comments to yourself. If you are sent for a bird, ask the 'gun' for direction as to where he thought it came down and, on collecting it, let him know.

Whilst beating in the line, keep pace with it. In thick cover the best way to do this is to keep in touch with the beaters on either side of you. Keep in touch with your dog also, and keep

131

him under control. This is not always easy as the birds build up in front of you and the noise and bustle around you and your young dog becomes more intense. The tapping of sticks, the cries from the beaters of 'Cock forrad' all around you as the birds get up, their shouts at their own dogs, together with the din as the 'guns' in your proximity let fly, can be very bewildering for a young dog. It is all too easy to lose contact with him in the general mêlée, so keep him working tight. It can be very embarrassing to hear someone out in front shouting, 'Who's dog is this running about?' It is also difficult to keep a young dog dropping to shot every few seconds as the shooting starts up at the end of the beat. It will seem to you that you are for ever saying, 'Gone away', and it is very tempting to forego this as you watch the casual way that the other beaters let their respective dogs rake on.

Always remember that these beaters' dogs have probably had the minimum of training and the maximum of experience. They know that their particular dog wouldn't pay the slightest heed to them anyway, and in many instances they haven't even the barest rudiments of knowledge of what a well-trained dog is. So regard your picking-up day as just another extension or progression of your training, and it will pay dividends in the end.

If your dog and you acquit yourselves well, you will be asked back. Furthermore word travels, and there is no advertising like word of mouth; good dogs being very scarce, you will get plenty of other offers to beat or pick up. I have found that, prior to entering a young dog in his first trial, a day or so picking up gets him used to crowds and to working in the company of other dogs. Crowd-shyness in a dog is more prevalent than most of us think, and a big shooting day can make a tremendous difference to a young dog in this respect, as well as really turning him on. I have on many occasions had a young dog or bitch who, whilst 'sticky' in the morning was going like a train by the end of the day, never to look back from that day on.

On being assigned a picking-up job, station yourself about 30 to 40yd behind your 'gun'. Let him know that you are there, and choose your stance carefully – a piece of rising ground is ideal. Await the commencement of action quietly. Do not move from the stance at any time, especially once the birds start breaking from the covert; it will not be appreciated if, by moving, you turn the birds back away from the 'guns'. Remember wildlife do not respond to a motionless figure, regarding it more as part of the surrounding terrain. A movement however will catch their eye immediately and force them to act evasively.

Note where the birds fall, if they are dead you can pick them later. The one to watch for is the high-flying cock. If you think he has been hit watch him until he is out of sight, but if after quite a long flight he suddenly rockets skywards and then falls, mark the fall, he is a dead bird. However, on the other hand, if a cock slowly loses height and lands perhaps at the perimeter of the field, he is most probably a very strong runner. If he is one of the early birds to break cover then you are in a difficult position, for if you move you may turn back any birds which are at that moment leaving the cover. At the same time if you don't get after him pretty smartish he will very speedily become an unpickable bird. This is very much a situation where you have to trust to your commonsense and the prevailing conditions. If there is obviously a lull in the shooting and not more beater-noise from the cover, then it is a safe bet to get after him as quickly as possible. If halfway across the field you hear a cry of 'Over', freeze; just mark that bird if it is hit and, as soon as things quieten down again, proceed after the original bird.

Always keep your young dog on a lead whilst standing behind a 'gun' – once again you are avoiding the potentially dangerous situation. If possible try to choose a 'gun' who is dogless, for if he has a dog with him he will most surely send it for every bird that he has down.

At the end of every drive make yourself available to the keeper for instructions after putting your birds in the game cart, he may still have birds down which have not been collected. And at the end of the day thank him for having you. Remember, if he is pleased with you he will ask you again.

MAKING ALLOWANCE FOR SCENTING CONDITIONS

Scent is not fully understood by anyone, it varies from day to day, even from hour to hour, and place to place. In a very small area it can vary from very good through patchy to very bad. Consequently, it is only possible to explain the known principles of scent and a dog's reaction to it.

First of all we must realise that wildlife survives through camouflage and sitting still; as soon as it moves it is at its most vulnerable. For instance a rabbit who has tucked into his 'seat' early in the morning will face into the wind so that the wind does not ruffle his fur, and consequently the area of scent given off is very small indeed. All wildlife tend to face into the wind and remain motionless until the very last moment. I am perfectly sure that, because of this, on the majority of rough shoots there is more game passed over than is ever found. It is for this reason that I have stressed that a dog must be under control, working a methodical beat, and allowed time to do it. In this way he will be given the chance to find the maximum amount of game.

In an area of just a few acres, scent can vary dramatically. For instance, a depression in the ground on a windy day will hold scent much better than the windswept area around it. Rushes hold scent well, as do any patches of bracken. As already stated, any extreme of climate is bad for scent, for example white frost before the sun gets onto it. But if late on a wintry afternoon you are hunting ground which was frozen in the morning but now has the sun on it, scent could be quite good, although that little area behind that bush with unmelted frost will hold little or no scent. Thus in only a few feet in this instance, the scenting conditions have altered from good to very bad. After torrential rain scent will be non-existent, a fresh fall of snow, will also cause bad scenting conditions. Gale force winds and heatwaves are weather extremes, and consequently scent in them will be very bad.

Moderation in weather conditions usually means a good scenting day. Experience once again is the great teacher, therefore if your dog is out with you one day and is working much slower than he normally would, pay special heed to the scenting conditions. A dog that possesses a good nose will react to changes in scent much more markedly than a dog with a poor nose. The following example will show what I mean.

At a particular field trial, conditions were as follows: a windswept hillside, therefore scent was poor; a strong easterly wind which made it even worse; the ground cover was heather under

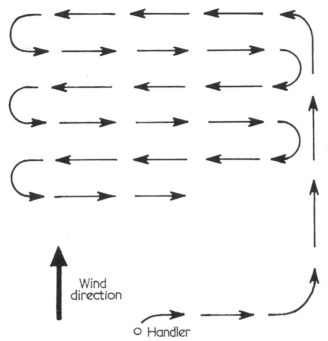

Wind
direction

○ Handler

Ground treatment: with a following wind (downwind beat) the dog will tend to pull out in front of his own accord. He should be allowed to do this and, with the aid of the recall whistle and turn-whistle commands, encouraged to work a pattern as in the diagram. The handler stands still until the dog has made the ground good back to him

melting snow, which was freezing again, virtually non-scent-holding cover in these conditions; the dogs were working on a down-wind beat; in other words dreadful scenting conditions. The dog that won this stake was actually charging about with his nose in the air, occasionally starting a rabbit because of the disturbance created by his activities. Rabbits were shot within ten or twenty yards of this dog, yet he had to be handled out to them, never once indicating any kind of scent. On at least one occasion he ran over the body and had to be handled back onto it. It was a clasic case of a dog without a nose and the judge concerned, by his placing him first, illustrated to all and sundry that he knew very little about scent. Almost all the other dogs in this stake worked their ground properly in the prevailing

135

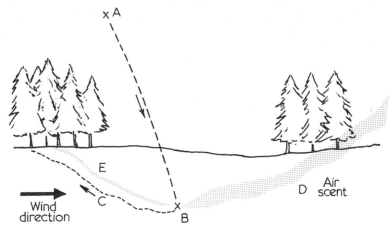

Scent in relation to wind direction: bird shot at *A* falls at *B* and runs to *C*. The air scent is quickly blown away to *D* and the dog will tend to take a line slightly downwind of the bird's foot scent (*E*)

conditions, ie slower than they usually did and much tighter to their respective handlers, with their noses on the ground.

You must make allowances for vagaries of scent; at all times be scent and wind conscious. If you school yourself in this habit and work your dog accordingly, the good experience he will gain will be the polish on the training. As time goes on your dog will gradually learn to adjust his hunting to your pace, consequently in a down-wind beat he will work his ground back to you in a methodical pattern. Remember it is just as easy to school a dog in good habits as it is to bed in bad habits, and the rewards are much greater.

Scenting conditions obviously play a big part in the handling of a dog to a blind retrieve. This is where an awareness of wind-borne scent helps greatly. For instance, supposing a rabbit gets up, unseen by the dog, with the wind coming from the left and that he runs straight out in front, is shot, and falls sideways into a ditch to the right. The dog has dropped to the shot, his eyes are upon you awaiting the command to retrieve, and you give the command, 'Dead. Get out.'

Normally you would be correct in doing this, for if your dog has been taught to take a line, in all probability he would hit the line and take it to the fall. But with a cheek-wind from the left,

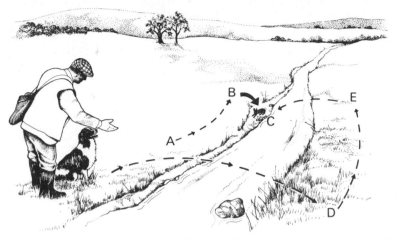

Rabbit gets up at *A*, is shot at *B* and falls over bank of stream at *C*. The dog is sent downwind to *D*, dropped, then redirected to *E* and dropped again. He is then handled into the wind, back across the stream

if you watched him on level terrain, he would probably line out to the rabbit by taking a line perhaps 3 or 4ft to the right of the rabbit's route – albeit an accurate line because he would get the rabbit. The reason he would be 3 or 4ft adrift is because very often a scent is wind-borne slightly down-wind, in this instance further to the right.

However, in the particular instance we are discussing, the terrain is not level, there is a ditch on the right, and the rabbit runs up the side of the ditch and is toppled into it. Therefore it is conceivable that if the dog does pick up the vestige of a scent, which is doubtful, on lining out he has nothing to work on at the other end, for the line is broken where the rabbit fell into the ditch. And remember, a dog does not trust his eyes nearly as much as his nose, so even if he looked down into the ditch he would probably not notice the rabbit. Furthermore, if you did what would come naturally to you in this situation, you would most probably drop the dog until you had his attention, then send him to the right with the appropriate hand-signal. In this case his natural reaction would be to jump the ditch and hunt the far bank, and on being dropped and sent back to the left he would become confused and a young dog would lose confidence.

137

The whole episode would be a failure because you were not wind and scent conscious.

It would have been far better, on shooting the rabbit, to put the dog over the ditch at the spot where you were standing, drop him on the other side, then send him up the far bank with the appropriate hand-signal. In this way he would either get a whiff of scent wind-borne to him or at least, if you dropped him as he drew level with the fall, you would be turning him across the ditch with his nose into the wind, thereby increasing your chances of a successful retrieve. The same treatment applies with a bird dropped unseen by the dog, stone-dead some way out in front of him. Always cast him off down-wind of the quarry and then work him up to it with the appropriate commands. Game falling close in to the leeside of a wall or any other wind-break will be almost scentless until the dog is on top of it.

Another tricky retrieve is a bird lying close in to the windward side of a wall or steep bank, in fact any depression in the ground will render it virtually scentless. This is because, the dog, to get down-wind of the bird, has to surmount the obstacle which will prevent the scent being wafted to him. Therefore what may at first glance look like a simple retrieve, may not be so. Game shot dead in the sky will fall with the minimum of disturbance, and if lying in a depression will give off very little scent. Try to be wind conscious.

You must try to assess each particular retrieve and the dog's reaction to it. Why did that retrieve look easy, and yet the dog made heavy weather of it? This is the only way to learn. I have seen two dogs 'down' on a bird lying on its back stone-dead in the furrow of a ploughed field, in perfect view of all the spectators and handlers, and yet both dogs in turn fail on it. But I expected them to, and was only glad that it had not happened to me. First the dogs had been hunting in rough cover of gorse and heavy dead bracken, secondly the bird had got up unseen by either of them, and was shot. You will discover with experience that it is extremely difficult to get a spaniel to handle out of good holding cover onto bare ground, so in this instance both dogs were probably wondering why they were being pushed out into the open, and consequently became discouraged all the sooner when they did not encounter scent. But never be too sure

138

of yourself, or too quick to criticise, it may happen to you.

Heather on a hot day in August, provides probably the worst scenting conditions imaginable, so bad in fact that I would most sincerely advise you against working an inexperienced questing dog on such a day. For the activity of the dog working in the heather raises clouds of pollen which choke him, and this can put a young dog off hunting for a long time to come. In these conditions an experienced dog is essential. However, I must add that nothing muscles a dog up more and gets him ready for the shooting season proper, than a few days at the grouse.

Any ground fouled by rotting vegetation, such as a carpet of leaves, will give off very little scent. Likewise thick, impenetrable cover will prevent the passage of wind and air currents, and thus scent will be poor. Hunting a dog on a warm day in gorse bushes which are still in flower, will mean that what little scent there is will be masked by that of the blossom to a certain extent. Wet, boggy, peaty ground, especially if it has an oily-looking appearance, with tall clumps of white grass, tends to send up dreadful fumes as the dog and yourself release the marsh gases as you proceed, thus virtually obliterating any trace of game scent.

Generally scent tends to be poor in the early morning, improves a little as the sun gets up, degenerates in the midday heat and then gets better as the afternoon progresses, reaching its best about an hour before sunset. The best scenting conditions are probably in the autumn when the weather tends to be moderate.

SUMMARY

1 Do not approach a keeper with the attitude that you are doing him a favour by offering to pick up.
2 On a bad scenting day allow the dog a little more time to work his beat.
3 Try to be wind and scent conscious at all times and work your dog accordingly.
4 It is just as easy to school a dog in good habits as it is to bed in bad ones.
5 Do not take an inexperienced young dog out shooting in heat-wave conditions.

CHAPTER TWELVE

Field Trials and Field Tests

FIELD TRIALS

If your dog hunts his ground in a workmanlike fashion at a good pace with his nose on the ground, within shot at all times, and does not require you to be constantly blowing whistles at him, retrieves to hand tenderly, can take a line and also handle out to a 'blind', if he is steady to fur, feather, shot and fall, then it is a fair bet that you have him up to trial standard, and may enter him in a field trial with every confidence that he will not let you down. This chapter outlines how to go about it, including the problem of pre-trial nerves and the preparation, or sharpening up of your dog.

Before entering your dog remember that, to give off his best, he must be at his physical and mental peak. There is only one way to achieve this, and that is to feed him on the finest food and exercise him like an athlete. He must not be too fat; at the same time, if he is too thin he will tire easily. A good guide is if at ten or twelve paces you cannot see the outline of his ribs, then he is about right. If you have been feeding him properly and giving him the additives as laid out in the early part of this book, plus adequate exercise, your dog should be fit for anything.

To perform at their peak, dogs require a high-protein diet and, whilst there are many excellent all-in-one dog foods on the market today, which are certainly very convenient and clean to use and which contain a high percentage of proteins and minerals, I have yet to come across one that could put the zip into a dog like nature's natural food in the shape of green raw tripe. This is undoubtedly a very distasteful, indeed nauseous part of the cow's anatomy to handle, and although on more than one occasion whilst standing outside cutting it with frozen fingers on a winter's night I have wished that there was a suitable substitute, I am certain my dogs do not, for they obviously relish it.

It is very easy to get up-tight as the date of a trial draws ever nearer. But remember, if you are over-anxious it will transfer to the dog. It is also very tempting to overwork the dog in the mistaken belief that you are getting him ready and improving his performance. Guard against this, for you will surely take the edge off him. This is a very common mistake with the amateur, especially with his first trial dog. It is unfortunate but nevertheless very true that, partly due to the media and partly to the attitude of some field trialists themselves, the ordinary chap has the mistaken idea that field trials are something very special, and that the participants are the élite. Nothing could be further from the truth. If the ordinary man who possesses one of the many dogs of good breeding, is prepared to apply himself to the training of his dog in a methodical fashion with the aid of a good text book in the off-season, he has nothing to fear in a novice trial. There are a few, thankfully only a few, who would like to keep trials a closed shop. On the whole, however, newcomers are welcome, field trials require new blood as any sport does, and it is a great pity if the would-be newcomer is put off by the erroneous idea that there is any difference between the training of a field trial dog to that of a shooting dog. There is no difference whatsoever. As already mentioned, if difference there be it is in the handler – one is a dog-man first, the other is a shooting-man.

Sharpening up Your Dog

For this, as in earlier work, it is desirable to have a friend with a steady dog to go shooting with. If you have not got this asset, or if your shooting companion's dog falls short in this respect, you have no choice but to go shooting on your own. We will deal with the solo excursion first.

You must conduct your shooting foray as closely as possible to the way in which you visualise a trial day will be conducted. On that day you will walk out to the judge with your dog on the lead; you will then be required to walk behind the judge until he is finished with the dog that is in the line at the moment. On being called into the line, you must sit the dog down and take

141

the lead off. He must remain sitting and all his attempts to fidget and get up must be discouraged, quietly. You may have to remain like that for a few minutes whilst the judge is making his notes on the last dog's performance. The judge will then stand up and tell you to hunt on; wait for him to tell you, do not assume that he is ready to commence. You will then hunt your dog as you would on a shooting day. Use your whistle as and when, but only when, necessary. Do not speak to the dog no matter what other handlers have been doing. Some handlers seem to be able to make as much noise as possible and get away with it, but do not assume that you will be similarly privileged – what may be tolerated from them may not be tolerated from you. Remember if you were out shooting and were making unnecessary noise, you would frighten the game. In a trial you will not only frighten game, you will be penalised for it. You must hunt your ground within shot methodically, missing nothing, drop to flush and shot, handle out to a blind retrieve if required, take a line on a runner if necessary and retrieve tenderly to hand.

Think about this, and the first thing that springs to mind is that it is essential to be quiet. Therefore if your dog gives tongue, forget him as a trial prospect. He must not speak either whilst on the lead, sitting waiting to hunt, or whilst actually hunting, for this will be severely dealt with.

It is an unfortunate fact that some judges tend to make speed the criterion in a hunting dog. Whilst I abhor a dog which is slow I do not judge a dog by speed alone, but try to get an overall assessment of a dog's performance in relation to the prevailing conditions. This is perhaps because of experience, bearing in mind that as a professional I am judging dogs of all grades every day of my life. I have now reached a stage where I do not assess a dog's capabilities as necessarily good because he is charging about at a breakneck pace. My first question with a dog like this tends to be, 'Is he a game finder?' If he is, well and good. Or is he rushing around because he knows no better or, because of being a puppy, is he rushing around for the sheer hell of it? Never take for granted that because a dog is going the fastest he is necessarily the best dog. Nevertheless, pace is important, you must endeavour to get the maximum from your dog that he may show to best advantage.

Macsiccar Cherokee, son of
field-trial winner Dumbro
Dally and field-trial winner
Macsiccar Merrit, a
stallion of his breed

Field-trial winner Macsiccar Merrit, a great hunter

The knack is not in the breeding of good quality but the recognition of it when you have it as a puppy

Field-trial winner Cherry of Macsiccar, a little bitch with a big heart

Various considerations arise in connection with this. If you hunt a dog hard all day, then, if he has even a modicum of commonsense, what does he do? He paces himself. He is used to being 'flogged' on all day, and adjusts his pace to conserve his energy, consequently he only goes at a fraction of his potential speed. Once you understand this you will act accordingly and begin to polish the dog. When you realise that in the majority of trials you will be extremely unlucky if you are under the judge for any longer than 20 minutes, you have your guideline.

This is the format for at least a month before a trial. You commence hunting your dog and you continue to hunt him for 20 minutes on good game-holding ground. This is most important; do not hunt a dog on unproductive ground if you wish to pep him up for a trial. During the hunting period, shoot over him, make sure of steadiness at all times. By all means let him have a retrieve, but restrict the retrieving as much as possible. Do the picking up yourself unless there is an interesting retrieve, for instance a 'blind' that you think he will benefit from. It is also a good plan to work the dog a little tighter than you would wish to work him in a trial. In this way he will take up a little more ground in the actual trial and still turn with the minimum of handling.

After a 20-minute period, put the lead on and walk him. Do not shoot during this rest or, as I call it, the frustration period. Walk him on the lead for 20 minutes, then commence hunting him again. This is the procedure from then on up to the trial date. I know it is very tempting when the dog is going like a bomb to extend the hunting period and shorten the lead period. Do not; if you resist the temptation it will be worth it in the end.

Some dogs do not require pepping up. This is a question that you will have to assess for yourself. However, the following is a good guide. If you can handle your dog easily and he is rock steady, then he can stand a pep up. On the other hand, if he is a hot piece of stuff and you normally have to be on top of him, you have no problem about pace. Therefore if you can give him a shooting day once a week up to the trial date to keep him on his toes, that will suffice. Never, never hunt a dog the day before a trial. If he is not ready for it, the day before will do little to correct him.

Preparing a dog in the duo situation is similar, the only variation being that it affords the opportunity of alternative retrieves. In other words, if your dog finds and flushes game he is kept steady on the drop, whilst your friend sends his dog for the retrieve. His dog on the other hand, will be kept steady whilst yours is retrieving his dog's finds. Not only is this a good exercise in steadiness to game and shot, it implants in the dog's mind that under no circumstances does he move whilst another dog is retrieving, nor must he interfere, squeak, fidget, or in any way be a nuisance. It also gives a dog valuable experience in handling out to a blind retrieve. This type of experience is desirable in the training of any dog; in the case of a potential field trial competitor it is of paramount importance. As to the 20-minute periods, these are just the same. Your friend may hunt his dog on, that is his affair, it could be argued that this would give your dog's lay-off period an added edge, which is all to the good.

If your dog meets the requirements laid down in this chapter, you may enter him in a novice stake without much fear of disgracing yourself, remember that whatever happens to you has probably also happened to the judge and most of the competitors. If you regard it all as a mini-shooting foray, and handle your dog as you would when out shooting over him by yourself, you will acquit yourself much better than you will if you take the whole thing too seriously. There is no one at a trial of any experience who will deride your performance. They are too busy worrying what Lady Luck has in store for them, to be bothered about criticising anyone else. True if your dog should run in, or be disqualified for some other misdemeanour, you will meet the 'experts' who will be only too eager to project their image by appearing knowledgeable and giving you all sorts of advice. I learned many years ago to listen and thank them for it, and then to forget it.

Trainers and Judges
Perhaps I have been unlucky, for through the years I have never encountered anyone in trials who volunteered good advice. What I have discovered is, that the people who know are usually the ones who tend to hide their light under a bushel. They tend

to be self-effacing and will not offer advice; but if you should, after having persevered in a few trials, begin to recognise these men – and they are very few – do not be afraid to approach them and ask their opinion, for if they give advice, it will be sound.

Do not fall into the trap of thinking that because a man is a professional, he is necessarily the best of trainers. In my experience this is just not so; indeed the two best trainers I have ever met are amateurs in as much that they do not train for the public. I remember approaching a professional many years ago and asking what I should do about a particular problem. He laughed and said, 'Train it'.

As I have said earlier, if you train your dog by the methods in this book you will know as much, if not more, than many of the pundits; therefore you have no need to place yourself in a position where they can ridicule you. Field trials have also got their fair share of amateurs who, by virtue of winning a couple of trials many years ago, have infiltrated into a little group of people who, not having any particular talent for the training of dogs, have nevertheless set themselves up as the élite, each in turn having his or her own little band of followers. Unfortunately, although thankfully few in number, this establishment carries a lot of weight. There are among them some who have never trained a dog in their life, some who have trained one or two and had some success, very often because they were liberal enough with their whisky in the right quarters the night before the trial. These people do, on occasions, judge trials.

Needless to say, never having shed much sweat in the training of dogs, they possess very little knowledge as to what is or what is not a good, bad, or indifferent animal. They are inadequates, who by honest means would not shine at anything. What makes me even more sorry for them is their pathetic lack of insight, their blissful unawareness of their own shortcomings. Unfortunately, however, they do damage to field trials, to their outcome and consequently to the breed. In some cases it is ignorance, in others it is downright dishonesty.

On the bright side, however, these people are far outnumbered by the honest judges. Therefore if you enter for a trial and are lucky enough to actually draw an entry number, the chances are you will get fair treatment, for the majority are men and women with a genuine love of the breed, and will give a dog its fair rewards. Therefore, do not be discouraged by what I have said. Bear it in mind though, for forewarned is forearmed. It will save you the disappointments and puzzlement which accompanied me for many years until I began to see what was going on. Never moan after a trial, it is neither the time nor the place. You are a guest on the ground and field trial societies have increasing difficulty these days in procuring sites. Furthermore, if you feel that you have had a raw deal don't bother asking the judge about it, for if he has twisted you he is hardly going to tell you. Do as I have done, improve your technique, and wait your time. The day will come when you will win and it is all the sweeter to know that you required no help to do it.

Before entering a field trial make sure that your dog has no faults. One fault is one fault too many. It will come to light and, as trials are over-subscribed and consequently difficult to get into, it is wasting not only your money but the judges' time. Also you are preventing a good dog getting a run. Nevertheless in saying that, I must add that if your dog goes at speed and has attained a satisfactory standard, then have no fear, if trials are your aim, enter him.

Entry Procedure

This is how to go about entering for a field trial. Firstly, remember that on being accepted as a member of a field trial society, you will be treated as a new member for six months. Consequently it is no use waiting until the trial season comes round before you join, for you will stand no chance at all in the draw, as new members' names do not go into the hat until the other members have been drawn. When you consider that for a 16-dog stake, it is not unusual for there to be 40 or 50 and even more entries, you will realise just how slim your chances are.

Let us assume that you have been accepted as a member and have been lucky enough to draw a number. You will probably have to travel some distance to the trial venue. If you are within reasonable distance, you may decide to save hotel expenses by travelling early on the morning of the trial. A word of warning may be helpful here. Although your dog may be a good traveller, you should remember that, for some time after getting out of a car, especially after a longish journey, many dogs, indeed the majority, will have after affects. Usually they have no nose, ie they cannot scent anything. This is due to the inevitable fumes of a car, undetectable to our senses but traumatic to those of a dog. Therefore if you have drawn a number say below 10, it is a good plan to travel the night before, letting the dog sleep in the car. They get quite used to this, especially if they have a good travelling box, and this way he will get out of the car the next morning fresh and raring to go.

Before breakfast, be sure to exercise the dog – 10 minutes is quite sufficient. Do not give him a training session, although no doubt you will see plenty of evidence of this going on all around you before the trial commences. This is quite unnecessary, indeed rather amusing. Except in my early days I have never indulged in it, believing as already said, that if the dog is not ready for the trial a fat lot of good practice is going to do him at that late hour. Take him out of the car and put his lead on. It does no harm at all to reassure yourself by patting the dog now and then, whatever you do, keep calm, at least outwardly.

Look for the trial secretary, he or she will most probably be giving out the armbands, the numbers. Introduce yourself and tell him or her the number that you have drawn. Thereafter join the spectators, that is unless you have been unfortunate enough to draw numbers 1 or 2, in which case you will be first in the line. I say 'unfortunate' because I personally do not like being drawn low in the stake; this is just my own personal preference however.

The Actual Judging

In a spaniel trial there are two judges, an A judge and a B judge, each having a dog in the line at the same time. One judge will take the even numbers, the other the odd numbers, one at a time until they have gone right through the card. As no. 2 dog is on the left of the line, no. 1 will be on the right.

Nearing the completion of number 1's run, the steward of the beat will signal number 3 to get ready. In which case number 3 will take up a position behind the judge, and probably beside the steward, until he is called under the judge. After 3 will be number 5 and so on. At the same time the judge at the other

149

end of the line will be working his or her way through the even numbers, but not necessarily at the same rate, for it all depends on how the game is distributed.

A judge in a spaniel trial is required to assess a dog's hunting capabilities, steadiness, and mouth. This is basically what your dog is being tried on, and the judge will try his best to keep you in the line until he has satisfied himself on these points. If you are lucky enough to go into the line and, after only a short hunt, get a find which is shot for you, and your dog makes a good job of the retrieve, you may well have a short run. On the other hand if you have no finds, the judge may keep you in the line for some time – it is just the luck of the draw.

The judge will walk beside you, but he will not interfere with the handling of your dog, neither will he speak to you unless to tell you where to hunt your dog, when to commence hunting, or direct you to send your dog for a retrieve.

You will find on entering the line, that there will be a 'gun' to your right and a 'gun' to your left. You are required to hunt your dog in front of both 'guns', but do not worry too much about this. As long as you give each of them a fair share of the dog's work, this is quite in order. But here a word of warning is useful – 'guns' at a trial are not necessarily dog-conscious. They are guests of the hosts, as you are; perhaps they are paying 'guns' in a syndicate and, as such, are therefore your hosts. They too may be suffering from trial nerves, thus may shoot badly in your opinion. Keep it to yourself. You may also find that one or other, or even both your 'guns' are wandering on ahead, thus interfering with your dog's pattern. Whilst this is very aggravating, you must not show it. It is for the judge to regulate the pace of the line; however you can take your own time and hope that the 'guns' will take the hint. This is just something we all have to live with.

You may from time to time hear shots from the other side of the line. Drop your dog every time. The judge will tell you whether to hunt on or not. During one of these intervals an exchange may go on between the judges. What is probably happening is either the dog on the far side has had a find and a retrieve but the judge wants it in the line a little longer, and therefore you are being offered the retrieve as you have not had one; or the dog at the other side has committed some fault or other. Whatever it is, the chances are you will be given the retrieve. Whilst you are not forced to accept it, you would require a very valid reason for not doing so. I have never refused, and it has done me no harm so far; so if you take my advice, accept it. But in these circumstances you are entitled to know exactly where the retrieve lies. Do not accept an airy-fairy wave of the hand and 'It's lying out there'. Ask exactly where it lies, and be sure before you send your dog. Experience will teach you when to accept the directions to the letter and when to deviate from them if you are in doubt.

Hunt your ground, work at it, do not proceed until you are sure there is no game on your patch. Don't take it for granted that because that bush is on the edge of your beat and the dog has turned before he got to it, that there is nothing in it. Put him in, make sure, remember you are on your own out there. Put him into every conceivable piece of cover that you think may hold game, for if he passes game you will be disqualified, or at best marked down so severely that you are out of the awards.

When the dog flushes game, use the stop whistle, short and sharp. In a novice stake a young dog may move on game as much as 4 or 5ft; you will not suffer for it, especially if he is going at a fair pace. If he is going fast and flushes on a down-hill cast he may even be allowed considerably more. However, in saying that, do not take it for granted, stop him.

You will be disqualified if your dog gives tongue, chases game, misses game, fails on a retrieve, damages game, runs into shot or fall, retrieves unshot game, 'pegs' game and does not let go on command.

If you have completed your first run, the judge will tell you to put your lead on, but he will not comment on your performance. You will then return to the spectators and await your turn under the other judge, unless of course you have been disqualified. Whilst in the gallery keep your remarks to yourself, be non-committal; no matter how well you think you may have done, play it down. You will feel extremely foolish if due to inexperience you misinterpret your performance, only to find that you have been disqualified.

Be attentive to what is going on. Keep your eye on the

steward for, due to disqualifications, your turn in the line may come a lot sooner than you think. If your dog is a bold, out-going character, he will probably 'hot up' whilst he is waiting. With this type of dog, no matter how keen you are to see the other dogs' performances, get to the back of the spectators and stay there. The ground that you are walking on has been fouled by the other competitors' feet and your dog's view of the pro-ceedings will be obscured; this will help to prevent him from 'hotting up' too much.

Should you complete your run under the second judge with-out blotting your copy book you may feel well pleased with yourself, for working a dog at trials provides many pitfalls. On the completion of their cards the judges will go into a huddle. They are making up the books, ie they are choosing the best dogs in order of merit by comparing notes. If may well be that they are in complete agreement, in which case the trial is over, except for the giving of the awards. However more often than not the judges, due to variable performances on the part of the top dogs, will require to see them run-off together to compare their style of hunting, drive, ground treatment etc. These are the all-important finer points, and a trial may be won or lost in these few vital moments. Usually the run-off consists of three or four dogs, but, the winner will not necessarily be among them. Very often a dog has acquitted himself so convincingly that he is 'on ice' – in other words, set aside.

The Awards

After the run-off everyone will return to their cars to await the giving of the awards. Usually there is a short time while the judges are signing the game book, award certificates etc, when you can relax, chat with the other competitors over the outcome, or have a cup of coffee. When all is ready the secretary will call you around and the awards will be announced.

Should you figure in the awards, perhaps get a certificate of merit as I did in my first trial, you may feel exceedingly pleased with yourself and your dog, for you are 'knocking on the door'. Should you even get into the money, perhaps reserve, third or even second, then you really have achieved something to be proud of. On the other hand should you win the trial, you will probably be asked to say a few words. This in itself can be quite nerve-racking. All you are required to do is say how pleased you are and to thank the judges; you may wish to embellish this, but my advice is, don't. The secretary will thank the host and make the appropriate sounds regarding the trial, 'guns' etc; make your speech short and sweet. You will then be besieged on all sides by competitors wishing to congratulate you.

I regard winning one's first trial with mixed feelings. If you are in this position remember this very sobering fact, that you are now stuck with an inexperienced dog who can only run in the big league. Also, it is very easy to get big-headed. Resist this, there are more than sufficient know-alls in trials without you adding to their numbers. Also remember that it will probably never be so easy again. In my opinion it is far better with a young dog to cut your teeth in a few novice trials, even running the whole of your first trial season in novice stakes, before winning and going on into the open stakes. In this way, not only will the dog gather valuable experience in the trial situation, but you also. If you pick up a couple of certificates and perhaps a place or two out of, say, six trials, then the chances are you have a trial contender in your young dog.

On the other hand, if you run your dog in the same number of stakes without an award, then you would be well advised to review his prowess. But bear this in mind that he may be too young or is, perhaps, a late developer. It may be that he will not blossom until his second season. Don't be too hasty in condemning him or too keen to win straight away.

FIELD TESTS

Providing that field tests are accepted for what they are, and are not confused or compared with field trials, I have nothing against them. Indeed if I had the time I would probably enter one now and again, but in a light-hearted way. If they fulfil a useful function, which is debatable, it is in the way in which they integrate a dog into the crowd scene. They may also give a novice handler a little experience in handling a dog in front of the 'gallery'. There the usefulness most emphatically ends, a field test is just that – a test – nothing more. They consist of a series of simple artificially devised tests or exercises, such as sending your dog for a marked retrieve, perhaps over an obstacle. In a spaniel test you will be required to hunt your dog for a few moments under a judge, and a shot will be fired to which your dog should drop. Simultaneously a dummy will be thrown which your dog should mark. Points are awarded on these exercises. In no way do they test a dog for steadiness to game, game-finding ability and, obviously, as the retrieves are artificial or cold game, cannot possibly test a dog's mouth.

It is a great shame that this innocent pastime has, over the past few years, been abused by a few to further their own ends. What I do not like about field tests is the unscrupulous use of the initials F.T.W. in advertisements either to sell puppies or to advertise a dog at stud. It has already been stated that a person who advertises a dog in this manner in an effort to 'con' the public is beneath contempt. It must also be said that if a person advertises a dog as having so many field test awards in an effort to impress, it begs the question. If he is so keen to impress why doesn't he advertise the dog's field trial awards? Obviously because the dog has none, or if the dog has run in field trials has not proved himself and consequently does not merit any special consideration when one is looking for a puppy or a dog at stud.

I would far sooner buy a puppy whose parents or parent had won a certificate of merit in a field trial, than a puppy whose parents were advertised as field-test winners. A field test proves only that the dog is proficient in the basics, nothing else. There are far too many people who, because they have won a test or two, regard themselves and their dogs as something above the ordinary. It is strange but nevertheless very true that not only does it take all kinds to make a world, but the humble dog has an uncanny knack of bringing out either the best or the worst in a person. If you wish to spend an enjoyable afternoon in competing in a field test, then by all means do so, but for goodness sake view it in its proper perspective.

CHAPTER THIRTEEN

Breeding

BREEDING POLICY

Breeding should never be taken lightly. You should always try to improve on the bitch that you have already got, or at the very least maintain the standard. Do not embark on a breeding programme with the idea that you are going to make a profit from the puppies. I think I can claim to being one of the first, if not the first, to advertise puppies at £50 each. That was in 1975 and, even although I never have any difficulty in selling my puppies, I have yet to make a profit. You are quite welcome to cost the enterprise at your first opportunity; I think you will be in for a big surprise. So why breed puppies, you may well ask. The obvious answer is to maintain a blood-line, if you are either a dedicated amateur or a professional, in which case you will approach the idea in a sensible manner. As always, when attempting anything new that is worthwhile, a great deal of thought and effort has to be employed if you are to make a success of it.

First and foremost no matter how sentimental you are about your dog or bitch, you do not, under any circumstances, breed in a fault. In other words, if you know your dog has a fault, you must not perpetuate it. If you do, it will most certainly appear in the progeny, and this will lead to dissatisfaction from the unfortunates who have purchased from you. This in turn will be broadcast, and no news travels like bad news. Consequently, your good name will suffer and in the future you will have difficulty in selling dogs, whether they be puppies or older animals. There is just no conceivable reason for breeding with sub-standard stock. Surely there is more satisfaction in knowing that you have, by a sensibly programmed breeding policy,

155

improved in some small way on what you started out with. Therefore, if it is apparent to you that your dog or bitch has a hard mouth, gives tongue, is gun-shy, temperamentally unsuitable for training or anything else which is inherent, you must not breed from it.

Furthermore if you, as owner of a dog, are approached by the owner of a bitch with the intention of mating the two, you must ask to see the pedigree first and should you, for one reason or the other, think it will be an unsuitable mating, you must say so. Remember, each time you mate a dog and a bitch you will have sparked off an entirely new line of life, which will in turn eventually begin several more new lines of life. Each line will have a new combination of propensities which will, to a greater or lesser degree, influence what comes after for the rest of time – quite a sobering thought, certainly not one to be taken lightly.

As time goes on you will gain new acquaintances in the dog world; no doubt you will on occasion see breeders accept bitches to their dogs purely with the motive of another stud fee. Let me assure you, they would make even more money if they went about it in an honest fashion. For if they were selective, the progeny could only improve instead of the good progeny being outnumbered by the bad, which has the effect of turning prospective bitch owners elsewhere for their stud-dog service. The breeding of dogs is like any other occupation. If you approach it in a fly-by-night attitude, you will not last very long. Conversely, if you are conscientious and deal only in quality, eventually there will come a day when your reputation will stand the test and you will benefit.

A great deal of thought must go into choosing a dog that will be suitable for a bitch, if there is to be any hope of success in the breeding. True, nature being what it is, no one can with any degree of certainty forecast the outcome of a mating. However you can be reasonably sure that, if you have a genuine desire to improve your particular blood-line, in time you will have fewer failures and more successes. Unfortunately over the past decade or so, good stud-dogs have become very scarce, at least so it would appear. No longer can one find in the field trial champions, the qualities of the great dogs of the past. One may well ask, where are the 'Rivington Glensaugh Gleans', 'Pinehawk Sarks',

'Markdown Muffins', 'Coneygree Simons' and 'Micklewood Storys' of yesteryear, to name but a few. These were the stallions of the spaniel breed, for they stamped their likeness upon their offspring. Alas they are no more, certainly their ilk have not appeared on the field trial scene in recent years.

What has happened to their kind, why have they disappeared from the scene? The answers lie in a large number of contributory factors. One reason is that with the advent of increased leisure-time and affluence, more and more people have taken up field sports and field trials, and the breeding of dogs is by no means the exception. By and large this is a good thing for new blood can only be to the overall benefit and continuation of the sport. Nevertheless, because of this increase in popularity, not all those indulging in the breeding of dogs have sufficient experience in what, after all, is a very specialised subject. Nor do they all, for that matter, care.

Evidence of this can be seen in the abundance of advertisements in the shooting publications proclaiming 'pedigree includes . . .' followed by a list of well-known dogs; or, 'sire field-trial champion so-and-so; dam, first-class working bitch'. All this is intended to impress and thereby encourage the public to buy the puppies, but it only illustrates all too clearly to the experienced dog-man that the owners of the bitches have gone to the 'named' dog of the day, with little or no thought as to whether the two are compatible or not. Thus over the past few years the spaniel breed in this country has produced more and more hypersensitive puppies and, unless a stud-force emerges within the next few years, the outlook will become progressively bleaker.

The prevalent policy of going to the top dog of the day with no thought to line-breeding or of a sensible outcross, can only result in pedigrees which resemble a hotch-potch of well-known dogs—a hit-or-miss affair. Would it not in fact be more sensible to go to the dog's sire, if there is a tie-in somewhere back in the pedigrees, for after all it was he who produced the dog in question?

A supreme example of the way everyone will start to use a particular dog to the exclusion of all others happened only a few years ago. A dog whose achievements in trials were of no particular note was used indiscriminately by all and sundry because

157

a trainer of great repute had said, 'That's the dog to use, it will put fire back into the breed.' Lo and behold within two years this dog's progeny were winning trials up and down the country. On the face of it, it would appear that the advice given was sound though I myself never used this dog, reasoning that if most of the good bitches in the country had been put to him, then surely he would be a pretty poor sire if if he did not produce some trial-winning offspring. It seemed to be an example of good advertising selling a doubtful product. What of the majority of the progeny, the ones that did not run in trials? It is obvious that there were, and still are, many of these around; in fact, it is now the exceptional pedigree that is without this dog.

But I have also found in the past few years that without seeing the pedigree but just by watching a prospective pupil retrieving (or rather not retrieving) I can tell a client that he has this particular dog in the pedigree more than once. True, they hunt and 'go' like hell's fire, but they are the most dreadful retrievers that I have ever seen, and on many occasions I have had to send his progeny home as unsuitable for training because of this. Few of us can afford much of that, so did he do the breed any good?

Certainly, a spaniel must be a hunter, but it is also essential that he should be willing to pick up. The spaniels in trials at that time may have lacked a little fire, but I have a suspicion that the ordinary shooting man would have preferred that. After all, the prime object of trials is to show the shooting-man the capabilities of certain blood-lines and to give him a yardstick. It is not to encourage a few cup-hungry people to breed spaniels to go faster and faster for the sole purpose of a twenty-minute run in a field trial, but whose progeny are so wild that the shooter dare not take his eyes off them for a second, even to take a shot. There were not many complaints in the retrieving sphere until this dog came along, but regularly now my phone rings and I am met with, 'Have you any pups, or have you a stud-dog without so-and-so in the pedigree?'

Everyone has to start somewhere. Like anyone else, I started out knowing nothing about breeding dogs. Through the years I have learned by trial and error and by and large my successful matings now far exceed the failures. I hope that by studying and applying my theories you will benefit from my experience in this fascinating subject.

There are those who will tell you that it is the dog which is the most important in the union. I do not, and never have, subscribed to this belief. It is rather curious and not a little amusing, to note that usually the people who expound this theory are the proud owners of a good stud-dog. I believe the most important factor is the bitch and that if you have a poor bitch, no matter how many top sires you use in successive matings, your poor progeny will far outnumber the good. I would far rather buy a puppy whose mother was a field-trial winner and the father of no note, than buy a puppy whose sire was a field-trial champion and the dam advertised as a first-class working bitch. For you only have the breeder's word for it that she is just that. Obviously, as she has just reared a litter of puppies, you cannot expect to see her prove her worth.

A first-class bitch can be put to a mediocre working dog and still produce quality puppies. What you must do is find a dog which you think has the qualities you are looking for, then look at his breeding. If this is similar, not too close, but with a tie-in to your bitch's pedigree you are far more likely to have good puppies than if you go to a Kennel Club champion who is an entire stranger to your blood. There must always be a common denominator. Even in an outcross you must still have, some-where back in the pedigree, a dog who is half-brother at least to a dog or bitch on the dam's side.

As mentioned in Chapter 1, it is the first three generations which have the greatest influence and consequently predetermine the future capabilities of the puppies. It is true that what may at first appear to be failure is not necessarily so, for whilst the desired quality may not appear in the first generation it may appear in their puppies. I believe that nature, with her sense of humour, reproduces every second or third generation, and have seen this happen time after time.

Let us assume you have a first-class bitch. Naturally you do not think that she could be improved upon but, remember, the perfect dog has yet to be born. Nevertheless, you would consider yourself twice blessed if you could just reproduce her, or at least almost her equal. Probably, after pouring over various pedigrees for weeks before she was ready for the mating, you finally choose a dog, a 'stallion of the breed', in whose pedigree, not too close, say about the third or fourth generation, there is a dog, or preferably a bitch, on the dam's side who is half- or even litter-brother or sister to a dog or bitch from the dam line of your own bitch. Naturally you expect to be onto a winner; you are entitled to. However don't be too disappointed if things don't work out just as you expect; as I have said, nature has a sense of humour.

But suppose you don't do too badly and you keep a bitch who although not being a patch on her mother nevertheless turns out to be good. In the fullness of time you once again find yourself searching for a sire, and think you have the right fellow for the job, always breeding to improve the quality of the progeny. It is in the litter from this bitch that you may well find a very close replica of your favourite. If not from this bitch then, with as near certainty as you can ever get in nature, it will come from one of her daughter's litters.

The knack, I have found, is not in the breeding of good quality but the recognition of it when you have it as a puppy. All too often you sell that little runt to some fellow who doesn't want anything special, just a shooting dog. You will probably eat your heart out if you should bump into him again in the future. I know, for it has happened to me all too often.

When you find the dog with the qualities you are looking for, if he is a field-trial champion well and good, for you cannot do better. But remember, do not be swayed by the fact that he is a field-trial champion. He is of no earthly use to you if the breeding is not suitable. Far better, if you can recognise quality, to go to the local shooting dog if the breeding is there. The only danger here is that you will have to rely on your own judgement in determining whether he has a fault which would be bred into your puppies. At least in going to a field-trial dog that has proved himself you have had this problem solved for you but, first and foremost, at all times bear in mind that you must have the tie-in. You cannot outcross forever, for this is a policy of pot-luck.

I believe in an outcross mating perhaps once every three generations. In this way you retain what you have got, and probably improve on it and strengthen the blood with the outcross.

160

No doubt, in time, you will encounter the exponents of 'Mendel's law'. My advice is to forget it, for you are not experimenting with plants. The people who propound this theory are usually keen breeders, but in the formative stage. Most breeders at some time or other give it a kick around for a short while, even if only as a theory, but they quickly realise that as far as breeding dogs is concerned it is not only too complicated but very much pie-in-the-sky stuff. Consequently, they abandon the idea. But at least it shows that they are prepared to give breeding serious thought, which to my mind is much better than the chuck-it-and-chance-it brigade.

COMING INTO SEASON

A bitch comes into season once every six months, first season probably occurring sometime in the first nine months of the bitch's life. I say probably, for it varies from one bitch puppy to the next, in some cases not occurring until as late as 15 months old. The season, or heat as it is sometimes called, lasts for 21 days, the fertile period being from the ninth to the fourteenth day; therefore the most propitious moment for successful mating is the eleventh day. However it is possible to fertilise a bitch at any time during these six days and, as a bitch's scent can carry a tremendous distance during this time, great care has to be taken if the unwelcome attention of marauding dogs is to be discouraged. The best plan is to keep her in kennel except for restricted exercise under close supervision and, if you are having trouble with stray dogs, spray entrances, around the doors, exits from your garden etc with one of the proprietary anti-mate sprays. These are readily available at any pet store, are extremely potent, and have a similar effect to tear-gas on any dog who comes too close. If you do not intend taking your bitch to the stud-dog, spray her also with this at the base of her spine, her tail, between her legs and underneath. Take care not to get it on your clothes or hands as it is not a pleasant smell and clings, as it is designed to do, for quite a long time.

Many people seem to have difficulty in recognising when the bitch is coming on heat, and tend to start counting the days

161

from perhaps the third day. Sometimes they do not recognise the condition until the bitch is 'standing'. It is really quite simple; here are a few pointers.

As the season approaches, many bitches become progressively more affectionate. Conversely they may become the opposite, ie whereas they have probably been very obedient and easily handled they become bloody-minded, hence the term 'bitchiness'. So be on the lookout for any dramatic change at or around the time you expect her to come 'on'.

The physical signs to look for are a very slight swelling of the vulva. If you should note this, gently part the vulva and you will see a very slight pinkish-coloured discharge. Around the third or fourth day you will have your suspicions confirmed. If then there is a marked swelling of the vulva, you may with confidence count from the first day.

Difficulty is also experienced in deciding when the bitch is ready for the dog. As stated above, the eleventh day is a safe bet. However, if you are in doubt as to when the first day really was, procure a dog from a friend and put him in with her. Stand and watch them; if she is ready, she will stand with her tail held high and to one side. The dog will also show a marked interest. There is now no time to lose; take her immediately to the chosen sire dog.

MATING

Mating dogs, especially if both dogs are inexperienced and the owners also, can be disastrous, in many instances resulting in a non-mating. This is primarily because:

(a) the owners get anxious and their anxiety transfers to the dogs;
(b) the bitch looks keen enough but on physical contact gives a yelp and jumps away from the dog, in some cases even snapping and growling at him. This can be quite off-putting, especially to a young dog;
(c) the bitch sits down and the dog loses interest;
(d) after successive failures the dog hots up and becomes exhausted.

Experienced breeders very rarely have much trouble with mating because they are calm. They know what to look for and what to do in every contingency. Perhaps the bitch is small and your sire dog is tall on the leg, in which case he will have difficulty, much more so than if it is the other way around. Even although both parties may be keen, they may have difficulty. The problem can be solved quite simply by holding the bitch, but whilst this is all right with an experienced sire dog, it may put off a young inexperienced one. The best way, if you don't know anything about it, is to put both dog and bitch in some enclosure where they cannot get out, but can romp about for a little time and, unbeknown to them, be kept under observation. In nine cases out of ten nature will overcome without human intervention.

If on your bitch's arrival at the stud-dog he shows no or very little interest, you are probably too early – if indeed your arithmetic is accurate. In this event do not sweat the dog. Arrange, if possible, to leave the bitch in a separate kennel for the night if you know and can trust the owner of the sire. Better still, take her back home and try again the next day. It is not unknown to leave a bitch with a breeder and on calling for her the next day be told, 'They were mated last night after you left; no bother at all.' But how do you know it was with the dog of your choice? If he is a popular sire and has had his quota of two bitches that week, that alone could account for the problem the day before, couldn't it? Wouldn't it be a simple matter for the owner of the sire to put the bitch to another dog who perhaps isn't so busy? Forgive me if I appear to be cynical, but I have known much worse skulduggery where money reared its ugly head. Play safe, avoid the potential danger, see the mating at all times, for it is the only way you can be certain.

A stud fee will be required for the services of a stud dog. His attainments or lack of in field trials, will determine the amount of fee asked. As a very rough guide, at the time of writing (1979) the fee for a Kennel Club champion would be around £60 to £65, although I know of one Kennel Club champion's owner who charges as much as £75. A field trial champion, that is a dog who has won two or more open qualifying field trials, would be around £50 to £55; good value, providing your bitch's pedigree and his have a common denominator to tie them in. The fee for a field trial winner approxi-

163

mately would be £30 to £40; once again good value. A dog with no qualifications can only be valued less than the above.

It is an unwritten law that if there is no issue from the union, you must get a return mating free of charge the next time, if you wish to breed from the same bitch. Some sire owners, if they like the look of your bitch, may request the pick of the litter as a stud fee, and this is perfectly in order. If you agree to this you must abide by it; personally I would far rather pay the stud fee.

After a mating, keep your bitch quiet in kennel for a few days. No violent exercise must be given. Furthermore, if you have a long drive home after the mating, take it easy with her. Don't try to break speed records, for it is not unknown for a bitch to ejaculate the sperm.

Incidentally, when the mating is in progress the two dogs will tie, ie they will remain together for a time, very often in a position where they are facing in opposite directions. Leave well alone; the longer the tie, the better the chance of a successful outcome. During this time the sperm is flowing from the dog to the bitch. Do not, as I have seen done, try to separate them for you may well do an injury.

CHAPTER FOURTEEN

The Next Generation

CARE OF THE BITCH IN WHELP

Gestation takes 63 days. There is very little danger should a bitch have her puppies as much as a week early, but on no account, under no circumstances, should she be allowed to go over her time. If she does, get the vet immediately, for in all probability you have problems.

There is a condition prevalent in puppies today, known as 'fading pup'. It has no specific medical name, for it is not clear just what it is, or what causes it. Consequently, treatment tends to vary from vet to vet, very often with very little chance of a successful outcome. So virulent can the condition be that I have known of instances where a kennel has had great difficulty in maintaining its blood-lines over a number of years, each successive litter being almost annihilated.

The first sign of trouble begins shortly after birth. The puppies set up a dreadful wailing which does not let up, and this squeaking will go on until they are all dead. The biggest puppy usually dies first, then the next in line, and so on until the very end. Usually, if one is saved, it will be the runt of the litter. Post mortem will show that, although these puppies were trying to suck and their mother appeared to have an abundance of milk, their stomachs are completely empty. The condition tends to manifest itself in particular blood-lines. However it is always a very real danger and well worth taking precautions before the problem arises, for if it does you are too late.

Although no one appears to have solved the mystery of this disease, my own personal theory is that it is of viral or bacterial origin. On many occasions I have noted that a bitch with small bare patches around her eyes, usually caused by the

165

Herpes virus, has produced a fading litter. It is feasible that this particular virus could be transmitted from the dog at mating, it could also be carried by a human being, ie if one had a 'cold sore', *Herpes simplex*. Obviously if you were suffering from this complaint whilst working with the bitch you would be extremely careful not to let her come in contact with it. Canine virus hepatitis could also be a primary cause, and it is therefore advisable to give the bitch her booster inoculation around the time that she is due to be mated.

Hypothermia, if present in the newly born puppies, is very often blamed if the litter fades. I myself do not consider it to be part of the fading syndrome; but certainly, if the temperature of the puppies is allowed to fall and hypothermia does occur, they will most certainly die, for as the body temperature drops all the vital functions slow down.

After being plagued by fading pup in successive litters for many years, and consequently having given it a great deal of thought, I have come to the conclusion that in the majority of cases it is caused by bacteria, the haemolytic streptococcus and staphylococcus being two of the most likely, possibly being transmitted by the dog to the bitch during the act of mating. Consequently, as a precautionary measure to enable preventive treatment to be used if required you should, within 3 days of the mating, get your vet to take a vaginal swab for culture and sensitivity. Should an infection be present, ie the culture is positive, the bitch must be treated with the antibiotic indicated.

The course of treatment will depend on the antibiotic required – ideally an initial injection followed by a 14-day course of tablets given orally. Then at the end of the pregnancy, approximately one week before the puppies are due, a further 7-day course should be administered. Since I inaugurated this type of treatment I have not had one instance of fading pup.

Normal exercise is the order of the day for a bitch in the first month of pregnancy. Indeed, take her shooting by all means; this will keep her in peak condition – she will not begin to show until about the fifth week. During pregnancy a normal balanced diet is essential; do not start pumping her full of food, a lean and healthy bitch will have a far easier birth than a fat and flabby one. During the second four weeks give her normal exercise, but be careful not to let her jump or squeeze through or under obstacles.

It is advisable to worm your bitch during the first few weeks after mating. Even though you may not see any signs of intestinal parasites in her droppings, or in her physical condition, it should be remembered that the round worms your bitch was plagued with as a puppy, went into a cystic form and entered her bloodstream when she was between 9 and 18 months old. They then become active again when she is pregnant, and enter the body of the foetus via the bloodstream.

WHELPING

For the actual whelping you will require a whelping box – a tea-chest will not do. This box should be approximately 4ft × 4ft × 4ft, open at the front and with a 9in board at ground level to prevent the puppies from wandering as they get more active. Clean sacking, one layer thick, should be nailed with broad-headed nails to the bottom of the box. You may have to remove this and replace it after the puppies are born, but it must always be spotlessly clean if cross-infection from other sources is to be ruled out. An infra-red bulb should be suspended from the roof of the box, approximately 3ft from the floor. In the last few days before whelping you will see your bitch become progressively more restless, scratching at the floor of the box. At this stage insert a few newspapers for her to tear up, and she will try to make a nest with these.

During the last few days of pregnancy step up the Adexoline (see Chapter 1) to approximately 12 drops per day. This will help the formation of bone in the puppies. Do not overdo the dosage or step it up sooner than 4 days before the bitch is due to produce her puppies, or you may find that they are so well developed as to make for a difficult birth.

As soon as you think the first puppy is due, take out the torn newspapers and replace them with layer upon layer of fresh, clean ones, laying them flat. From now on, if and when you find it necessary to visit her, approach her in a quiet manner and be calm. Keep all external noise to a minimum. Tell the children to play elsewhere, if she gets peace and quiet she will get on with

167

the job by herself. However any strange noise may cause her to stop in the middle of the litter, and I have known a bitch delay the delivery of the remaining puppies for as much as twelve hours because of an unusual disturbance.

As the puppies arrive, remove the soiled newspapers one by one, leaving the mother with a dry surface. At this stage be on the look out for a green discharge, and if this is noted, get your vet immediately. There may be a dead puppy inside her; at the very least there are probably complications in the offing. Do not, once the puppies start appearing, be continually going into her. Leave well alone, do not handle her puppies, and do not have friends popping in to see them until they are at least a week old.

The duration of delivery varies between bitches but, on average, a puppy should appear at $\frac{1}{2}$ to 2 hourly intervals. If there are obviously still some puppies to come, and there has been an interval of more than 4 hours, get your vet. There could be a puppy blocking the birth canal, in which case it is a job for the expert. On the other hand it may just be a simple matter of an injection of Pitocin. However, you must leave this to the vet.

Once the puppies are delivered the bitch will settle down and lie quietly. She may or may not desire to eat during the first twenty-four hours, many bitches don't. She will have eaten the placentas as they appeared with each successive puppy; she must be allowed to do this, it is nature's way, and they contain hormones which help in milk production. If she does not want to eat, do not worry; it is essential however to have a plentiful supply of clean, fresh drinking water available for her. If the puppies are quiet, they are contented and well-fed. Watch any puppy that she discards, for this is a poor doer and will die. In this again it is better to let nature take its course.

If the puppies are well oxygenated their noses will be a nice shell-pink colour (blueness denotes hypothermia). If when you place your hand on the sacking (you should have removed the last of the newspapers after the last pup was born) you find it is pleasantly warm but not hot, the puppies are getting enough warmth. If not, lower the bulb a few inches but be careful not to overheat, 3ft above the floor should be low enough for the bulb to do its job.

From now on feed your bitch well, with small but frequent feeds, and on high protein with the addition of milk and eggs plus additives. The quality of the puppies will be determined by how well you feed her.

Of late there has been a great deal of controversy regarding the docking of puppies' tails. Unfortunately the world today is full of do-gooders, for they have little else to do. The anti-docking brigade think they are doing good, but as is usually the case with do-gooders they are motivated by ignorance and the belief that they must be right. Without going too deeply into this, let me just say that it is far more cruel to leave a tail undocked on a hunting dog, owing to the damage done to it in rough cover, than it is to perform a very simple and *painless operation.*

The method I use is believed to have originated in the famous Rivington Kennels not far from me at Castle Douglas, and is completely painless and bloodless. When vets can be seen cutting puppies' tails with a resultant blood-bath, and then stitching them up, no wonder the do-gooders can put up a case for cruelty, but I have on many occasions docked a puppy's tail whilst he was asleep, and he has continued to sleep – obviously not much cruelty is involved.

The tool used is very simple to make but well worth it. Take a piece of mild steel $\frac{1}{8}$in thick by 2in long and 1in broad, and sharpen one end with a reaper file until the edge is obtained. This is then honed on an oilstone to a sharp cutting edge. A rod ($\frac{1}{2}$in round bar is ideal) is then slotted over the other end of the blade and welded, and a wooden handle attached for a grip. The whole tool when assembled will be approximately 1ft long from the handle to the cutting edge.

When the puppy is 4 days old is the time to dock the tail. Do not delay, as the tail gets thicker as time goes on. Lay the docking tool on the hot plate of your domestic cooker with the cutting edge on the element, until it is hot enough to brown a piece of newspaper when laid flat on it. As soon as this degree of heat is reached, dock the tail and lay the tool back onto the hot plate in preparation for the next puppy.

169

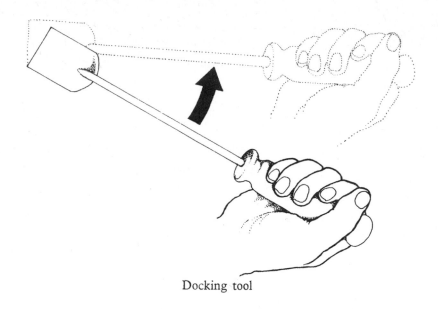

Docking tool

To dock the tail, hold the puppy around the body gently but firmly. It is better to enlist someone's aid to do the holding, as you will have to hold the tail with one hand as you use the other to hold the docking tool. Place the puppy's tail on a block of wood about 2in thick. Holding the docking tool rather like a dagger, lay it in line with the site where you wish to make the cut, touching the block of wood with the corner of the blade so that by a swift, forward motion it will slice through the tail with one stroke. In a working spaniel it is desirable to leave two-thirds of the tail on. Nothing looks more ridiculous than a spaniel with the tail shorn off. You will find that, using this method, there is no pain if you execute it with a swift, firm, downward stroke very like the stroke of a chisel, not with a cutting stroke such as you would use to slice bread with a knife. There should be no blood at all if the site is correct. However if you are slightly high on the tail or if the blade has cooled slightly, a spot of blood may appear at the end of the tail. Quickly lay the flat side of the blade against this to cauterise it, and there will be no further bleeding. Heat the blade after each puppy has been docked. Do not use it unless it is hot enough to brown the paper. You will find that this is the most humane method you will ever encounter, and certainly there is no need to feel squeamish about it. After you have done the operation for the first time you will find it simplicity itself. It may help to have a mock run if you are not sure of the instructions.

When removing the puppies from the 'nest' for docking it helps to get the bitch out of the way for a few moments while you take half the litter, and again when you are returning them. If the kennel is outside, have a cardboard box containing a hot-water bottle wrapped in a towel, to carry the puppies in. Cover this box with another towel to protect them from draughts.

It is strange but very true that there are more puppies lost through cutting dew claws than docking tails, consequently I would advise you to leave this operation to the vet. However, I rarely remove dew claws unless they are a deformity, and have never encountered, for all the dogs that I have trained, a single one who tore his dew claw off, or had a dew claw which grew around into the leg. I do not doubt that it can happen, only that it is as common as some authorities try to make out. Therefore, my advice is, if the dew claws are not abnormal, leave well alone.

WORMING AND CLAW TRIMMING

Puppies are born with intestinal parasites from their mother's blood stream, and at or around the 4 week old stage these worms are reaching maturity. They will now absorb the nutrients from the puppies' food, with the result that their condition will degenerate. Nowadays it is a very simple matter to deal with these parasites. Once again, I can recommend Shaw's Early Worm (see Chapter 1) which is the forerunner, if you like, of Shaw's Everfree. This particular product may be used with complete safety at the age of 3 to 4 weeks old before the worms can do much damage, though with any other product it is better to wait until the puppies are 6 weeks old unless stated otherwise. Administration is simplicity itself. Place the thumb and forefinger over the puppy's muzzle, gently squeezing the jaws open while at the same time holding his head tilted back. Pour the prescribed dosage off the spoon, letting it trickle over his gullet – as it has a chocolate flavour the puppies take it quite readily. Results, even in puppies who have shown no outward signs of infestation, are usually quite dramatic.

171

At around the 3 to 4 week-old stage your puppies' claws will be getting quite sharp and may be causing the bitch a great deal of discomfort whilst they are feeding; therefore it is quite in order to trim them back a little with an ordinary pair of nail scissors.

At 5 weeks old the puppies are ready to be weaned. For the first two days teach them to lap; this is easily achieved simply by taking each puppy in turn and placing a saucer of Sherley's Lactol (available at any good pet shop) on the floor in front of him. Some puppies will start almost immediately with little or no encouragement, but in the majority of cases a little tuition is necessary. By dipping your finger into a warm Lactol – which must not be warmer than blood heat – and holding the puppy's nose close to the saucer, encourage him to lick your finger; within a few seconds he will be lapping as though he had been doing it all his life.

Do not overdo the quantity of Lactol, half a saucerful is more than sufficient at this age when they are also still on their full quota of bitch's milk. After you have the puppies lapping, it is a simple matter to give them two meals a day like this, until the beginning of the sixth week, when you should introduce them to a little minced cooked meat, preferably warm but not hot cereal and milk or Lactol, egg and milk and a little all-in-one meal. But once again err on the small side rather than give too much, and this type of meal must be thoroughly moistened, much more so than it would be if given to an adult dog. Puppy biscuit can also be given at this age.

By the end of the sixth week you should be able to remove the bitch for the whole of the day, only allowing her into the puppies for 10 minutes in the evening. The puppies must be completely weaned by the end of the seventh week, and on no account must they be allowed near their mother at any time after, for if you allow them near her she will begin to lactate again. Under no circumstances must this be allowed to happen.

The puppies should now be having five meals per day or, alternatively, be fed ad lib from a hopper with a good all-in-one puppy food. When using this method I also give a milky meal in the morning and fresh meat in the evening, giving the additives (see end of Chapter 1) with one of these meals.

From the moment that you take the bitch away from her puppies, start giving her daily exercise, stepping it up each day until she is back to her pre-natal fitness. During this time be careful to keep her away from heavy cover such as brambles until her under-carriage has fully tightened up.

SELLING A PUPPY

You are duty bound to give a pedigree with each puppy, furthermore, this service should be free. Lately there has been an ever increasing trend for breeders to advertise puppies at such and such a price, and then when the client comes for one they try to charge extra for a pedigree. This is just not on.

Try to place your puppies well, ie try to judge the character of the client. A lot can be learned from the latter's remarks whilst he is looking at the puppies. Do not be lazy when it comes to writing out the pedigrees, write them out by hand. When you have seven or eight puppies this can be a very laborious and tedious job, but it is all part of the service; to give Photostat copies does not encourage clients to have a good opinion of you.

Try to build a good reputation, it pays in the end.

Index

Page numbers in italic type indicate illustrations.